MODERN WEALTH BUILDING FORMULA

How to Master Real Estate Investing

KEN VAN LIEW

TK GLOBAL PUBLISHERS, LLC

NEW YORK * ATLANTA * LOS ANGELES

Modern Wealth Building Formula™

Published by:

TK Global Publishers LLC
954 Lexington Avenue
New York, NY 10021

Printed in United States of America
First Edition: November 2019

Catalog-in-Publication Data for this book is available from the Library
of Congress
Library of Congress Control Number:2019917326

ISBN 978-1-7338004-3-3

PRAISE FOR MODERN WEALTH BUILDING FORMULA

"I know a billionaire that used Ken's Formula, Listen to this guy, real estate equals success."

- Jack Canfield

Cocreator of the Chicken Soup for the Soul Series

"When you see the legacy Ken built in New York City, it's astounding! If I was wearing a hat, I would take it off to him."

- Dolf de Roos

New York Times and Wall Street Bestselling Author, Real Estate Riches

---

"The secret to success in wealth building is deconstructing the complex, and creating a simple blueprint to follow. Ken is a magician when it comes to this! He has engineered a process that will allow you to realize the same level of success that he has experienced. Well done Ken!"

- Carl Gould

#1 Bestselling Author, International Entrepreneur of the Year

---

"I have known Ken Van Liew for close to 30 years, when he managed the reconstruction of 1.2 MSF of Class A office space for Prudential Securities at One New York Plaza. As a close friend, I have watched Ken's career grow as he developed real estate for the largest owners in NYC, and for his own account. His meticulous attention to detail, from value engineering the design and components of a $100M project, to rescuing developments from mid-construction challenges, demonstrates his uncanny ability to leverage his experience and relationships to solve problems. He has shown how to create a critical path action plan for real estate success, that is utilized by some of the most successful players in this arena. His book is a valuable tool for those who want a deep dive into the mindset and game plan to have significant success in real estate investing."

- Richard Van Houten
President Van Houten Group

"With 90% of millionaires becoming millionaires through real estate, why not increase the already irrefutable odds with a formula that shows you how to build lifelong wealth? You learn from the top down with a new paradigm to perform every type of real estate investing."

- Divya Parekh
9-time #1 International Bestselling Author

"When we met, Ken and I laughed about our alma mater and winning high school championships decades apart. With hometown spirit, a new friendship and a substantial return investing with Ken, he inspired me to build my own portfolio in real estate. His book was perfect timing and just hit my sweet spot. Touchdown!"

- LJ Smith
Entrepreneur & former NFL Philadelphia Eagles Tight End

"Having known Ken for over 20 years, I can truly attest to his brilliance in business and real estate. In the Modern Wealth Building Formula, he breaks down the immense value of real estate investing and generously shares his knowledge and strategies. Whether you are about to begin as a new investor or want to take your investing skills to the next level, this book will provide the insights and master plan to do so. Modern Wealth Building Formula is truly a must read for anyone who wants to build wealth through real estate."

- Leanne Gabriel, Esq.
Entrepreneur and International Speaker

"We all want to model success and wish we had the formula. That's just what Ken Van Liew delivers in this easy to digest book. Read closely and take action!"

- Jess Todtfeld
Former TV Producer at NBC, ABC & FOX

"My relationship with Ken Van Liew has stretched over more than 25 years. We started as attorney client and over the years have evolved into personal friends. Ken is an accomplished construction professional and licensed engineer. He has the ability to build anything from skyscrapers to backyard sheds and everything in between. When thinking of Ken several words immediately come to mind such as smart, insightful, dedicated, loyal, resourceful and others. I have represented Ken in all manner of real estate from acquisition, financing, disposition, leasing and almost anything you can imagine. I have also found him to be knowledgeable, professional and single minded in getting the project done and maximizing everyone's value in the project. It's great that Ken has finally decided to share his knowledge through this book. I'm sure it will be a smash hit."

- John R. Frieri, Esq.
Founding Partner of Frieri Law Group, LLC

"Ken is a lifelong dearest of friends who above all is a person that is always there for you when needed. His drive and creativity for developing real estate wealth success strategies have endured time and the cyclical behavior of the markets."

- Robert Nawy
CEO, IPKeys Technologies

"Ken is one of the smartest construction strategists and influential real estate advisors in the business. He is a master of organizing multiple projects simultaneously, implementing effective systems and executing with precision. I've observed his consistent brilliance on our corporate headquarters development, formerly Lehman Mansion, Millionaires Row, New York City, land dispositions, penthouse and residential developments while minimizing our risk and protecting us against construction claims. Little did I know, I've been benefiting from his formula for many years and now you will also."

- Craig Lucas
Hedge Fund Manager

"The *Modern Wealth Building Formula* gives the everyday investor a simple understanding of real estate investing and a shot at getting in the game."

- Steve Harrison
Co-Founder of the Quantum Leap Publicity and Marketing Program

"Ken Van Liew is a self-made, real estate and peak-performance expert who tells it straight, lives to the highest standards of character and integrity, and is committed to helping others. I've been investing in real estate for almost 35 years and when I have a question, Ken is the *first* person I call. I am blessed to have him as a business partner, and to consider him a dear friend!"

- Bob Quintana
Entrepreneur. Advisor. Investor., CEO/Founder – RLQ Consulting Group

---

"When you think of successful real estate moguls in NYC, you may picture someone ruthless and arrogant. Ken is neither of them. Not only is he brilliant and methodical, his compassion and willingness to make sure you are successful while using his programs is genuine. Whether you work with him through his online courses or privately, using his years of hands on experience, he brings a unique perspective on successful real estate investing which is invaluable. I highly recommend you dive into his book or any of his other programs and just know, you will be successful when you fully follow his lead."

- Dr. Phil Agrios
International Personal & Business Consultant

"In this inspiring guide, revealing the proven formula for success in real estate investing, Ken Van Liew shares his years of experience and industry knowledge to provide readers with practical information and strategies to create lasting financial freedom and security. He has created a simple system that anyone can easily follow, even if they're new to real estate investing."

- Renee King
Marketing and Publicity Consultant and Author

"Ken's *Modern Wealth Building Formula* not only gives you a cutting-edge advantage in any real estate market, it's the foundation for any business providing extensive value to the beginner, intermediate or advanced investor. This is a must read as it dissects the investment process into three easy steps - Find, Find and Facilitate to accelerate your success in real estate."

- Ross Hamilton
CEO Connected Investors

"Without even opening the book, I already knew it was going to deliver big time! I've known Ken for years, and not only has he taught me a lot about Real Estate, I know I can count on him to deliver in detail and not skip any part of the process. Ken does not disappoint. When I read the **"Modern Wealth Building Formula"**, I knew it was not just another book I would leave on my shelf. And to know that someone like Dolf de Roos honored the forward, enough said!!! From someone that bought their first property in 1991, and has done over 150 deals, I've learned one of the most important components of Investing is your network. Your network can make or break your Real Estate career. Ken is definitely a guy to know if you want to explode your Real Estate Investing career!"

- Ken Spohn
The Real Estate Ninja Coach

"A large number of the wealthy people I have connected with over the years have created their wealth thru real estate. If you want to model someone who has create lots of wealth thru real estate do yourself a favor and pick up Ken Van Liew's book Modern Wealth Building Formula."

- Larry Benet
Chief Connector

"I have had the extraordinary privilege to have known Ken Van Liew for over a decade and I consider him a dear friend. He wants everyone around him to win and that's the heart of a great transformational leader. Ken is one of the few I know who has the ability to demystify the complexity of real estate investing and make it fun. If you are committed to leveling up, tap into Ken's wealth of knowledge and experience with his Modern Wealth Building framework and programs."

- Joseph Varghese
The Breakthrough Engineer, Founder of Success Circles

QUESTIONS:

- Do I need to be a millionaire to invest in Real Estate?
- Can I invest in Real Estate without experience?
- Do you want to know how to get more time?

ANSWERS:

Sign up for a FREE
45 minute strategy call at
www.kenvanliew.com

DEDICATION

I would like to dedicate this book to my wife, best friend and soul mate, Terry! To our children, Michael, Alyse, and Courtney. And to my brother, Paul, and Mom and Dad for all their unconditional love, enthusiasm, and vision to create unlimited possibilities in life.

CONTENTS

ACKNOWLEDGMENTS

My enthusiasm about life and my passion for real estate have led me on this amazing journey to offer my knowledge and experience to others in the hope that we can all come together to form strong entrepreneurial ventures which can provide for our families for many generations to come. It is my sincere desire to create a thriving community of partnerships with future business relationships which will help us all move toward successful real estate investments.

Without the guidance from many mentors, trainers, clients, friends, associates and a few select professors, I would have never reached my goal of bringing this book to life. I offer my sincerest thanks, gratitude and acknowledgement to all of you for believing in me.

While it is impossible to acknowledge everyone, many people deserve and have my deep appreciation for keeping me on track throughout this journey. If I missed any of you, I apologize in advance. First of all, I would like to thank my family for their ongoing patience, support and encouragement during my book writing process. Especially my wife – honey you are my rock, without you none of this would be possible!!!!!

A deep thanks to Jack Canfield, Tony Robbins, Dolf de Roos, Rich Kelly, Grant Cardone, Daymond John, Lisa Sasevich, Divya Parekh, Carl Gould, Steve Harrison, Jess Toddfeld, Justin Spizman, Mark Surkis, Rick Frishman, Lucas Garvin, Jaison Varughese, Craig Lucas, Eric Brody, Phil Agrios, Larry Benet, Adam Giandomenico, Perry Yeldman, Ross Hamilton, Geoffrey Berwind, Martha Bullen, Raia King, Richard Van Houten, Ed Leybovich, Ken Spohn, John Frieri, Ravin Jagoo, Mace Smallwood, Theresa Klekar, LJ Smith, Jeff Glasco, George Arroyo, Lee Smith, Dan Sobel, Naveed Bhatti, Dr. Phil Agrios. I have found so much inspiration and support through your words, influence and teachings.

A NOTE TO THE READER

Dear Reader,

If you've picked up this book, you have taken the first steps to empower your future through building a wealth portfolio for real estate development and investing. As you read this book, you will find a better way to create a much more fulfilling and prosperous life through lucrative real estate investment opportunities. Maybe you are interested in real estate and considering a second stream of income, or you might just be looking to punch your ticket into the real estate industry and invest your hard won earnings into smart and profitable income sources to accelerate and grow your existing wealth. In any event, this is the book for you. There is a wonderful wealth of knowledge available to you that can offer you the insight and crucial training to get the inside track on real estate.

Many of you may have arrived here with a developed interest in real estate investing and would like to learn more—discovering how you too can be successful in the real estate market. This book will give you that. But I will work to take you even deeper into the real estate industry, explaining the vast prospects residing in the real estate market — from commercial to residential, new builds to fixer-uppers, skyscrapers to single-family homes, and much more. These are all not only available to you, but each offer their own intrigue and pros/cons. Together, we will explore each at length so you can make the right choice to suit your own preferences and tastes.

Whatever your story may be with money, business and life, you've come to the right place. I'm here to help. I've experienced the self-defeating talk around savings, investment and your future. The truth is that I've made the money, lost the money and then made it again. I will share with you my story of how I overcame these challenging patterns and ups and downs to eventually derive my formula for success across the real estate market.

It was only after I applied my experience in engineering, years of studying the market, and hands on real estate experience that I became an expert in real estate investing. And with the relationships I have formed with the experts in the fields, what I don't know is only a phone call away. Herein, I will teach you how to find sources to support your desired outcomes and build a valuable and impactful portfolio grounded in the real estate market.

Wherever you are in your journey, I look forward to supporting and encouraging you along the way. Through the wisdom I have tried to incorporate into this book, you will find your path to financial security, while enjoying the passionate pursuit of a tangible investment that actually means something to the world. There is little more gratifying than seeing your hard earned dollars offering you a return in the form of a single-family investment property or even a large skyscraper in the middle of the city. No matter your taste or risk tolerance level, this book is an excellent first step, and I'm happy that you have chosen to read the Modern Wealth Building Formula. I'm honored to be part of your journey and look forward to our journey in learning together.

It is my privilege to meet you, and I sincerely hope we can create and continue a conversation. You can contact me at kenvanliew.com/connect/. Please visit www.kenvanliew.com to explore possibilities.

With sincere gratitude,

Kenneth J. Van Liew, P.E.

CONNECT WITH KEN AT:

https://www.linkedin.com/in/kenvanliew/

https://www.facebook.com/kenvanliew/

https://www.twitter.com/kenvanliew/

https://www.youtube.com/KenVanLiew

FOREWORD

by

Dolf de Roos, PhD

Most people involved in real estate agree that nearly anyone can excel investing in property, as the industry is very forgiving of mistakes. Indeed, almost every home owner in America (and most of the world for that matter) has done extraordinarily well with their "unintentional investment" of owning a home, and the most frequent lament you will hear from retiring home owners is, "If only we had also bought a second home, or better still, ten or twenty of them, and a commercial building!"

Nonetheless, despite the relative ease with which most investors do well, very few end up owning ten or twenty homes, let alone a commercial building. Even fewer end up building over one billion dollars of real estate.

This is precisely why Ken Van Liew's story is so extraordinary, and why there is so much to learn from reading this book.

Unlike many big-time players in the real estate market, Ken didn't start with a hefty loan from a relative, nor was he given an existing portfolio to manage in order to "learn the ropes". Rather, he had an initial interest in civil engineering and site design, which led to an intense desire to learn real estate investing and development. A severe dose of enthusiasm along with an indomitable spirit propelled him to heights of which most people only dream.

I first met Ken in 2001 when I delivered a presentation on commercial real estate in New York City. Like many participants, he hung around to speak with me at the end. But rather than ask me questions, he said that what I had talked about gelled so much with his own philosophy and strategies that he couldn't wait to show me around his mini-empire, the crown of which back then was his recently completed

$17 million Assisted Living facility. His enthusiasm was contagious. It was probably inevitable from day one that we would become friends.

But I didn't get to see his empire then – I was on a tight speaking tour schedule. Over the next six or so years, I traveled the world, teaching real estate investment in 26 countries, publishing 15 books, and growing an international brand. Ken, meanwhile, continued his path of investment and development in the New York Metropolitan area. We stayed in touch. A seed of cooperation was planted, but we didn't act on it at first.

Around 2008, I visited Ken again in New York City, and finally got my tour. We marched all over Manhattan, from tenement buildings that he was consolidating in order to create a high-rise site, to vacant land that had just been cleared, to buildings under construction, to finished condominium towers where the penthouse was on sale for $20 million. This was hardly a "mini" empire!

We visited The Richmond, his 24-story development, featuring 100 luxury condominiums at 80th St and 3rd Avenue. I was blown away by its scale and innovation. From there, we went to 300 East 64th St, where his development encompassed 103 units spread over 27 floors. And to another at 1055 Park Avenue, which was featured on *Million Dollar Listings* on Bravo TV. Crucially, these projects also incorporated major ground floor retail tenants, including Bank of America, Chase, United Artists Theater and Starbucks, to name just a few.

We visited his recently completed 240 Park Avenue South, featuring 52 luxury condominiums. From there, we were chauffeured to Brooklyn, NY to see the three million square foot Metrotech Center that included the Securities Industry Automated Corporation providing daily back-up for every New York and American Stock Exchange transaction, the Brooklyn Union Gas Headquarters with an amazing two level real-time electronic mapping grid of the entire gas distribution system in the five boroughs, and the E-911 Emergency Command Call Center developed under his direct supervision. Clearly, Ken was a machine!

Throughout this tour, I was struck by two things about Ken… First, everywhere we went, without exception, everyone from site foreman to drywall carpenter to building manager was genuinely excited to see him. And while he showed me around, gesticulating with his hands and smiling broadly, he would nonchalantly hold a ladder while someone climbed it, pass a power tool to someone, or give a suggestion as to how something may be done better, all without skipping a beat in our own animated conversation. I felt like I was on the set of a tightly scripted and choreographed commercial. The second thing I noticed about Ken, was that he was constantly talking about new innovations and ideas that kept his product ahead of the competition. To excel in business (especially New York City real estate development), it is not sufficient to merely copy an idea that is working now, because as the world rapidly changes, that idea may no longer be desired or appropriate for the market. Most people just copy the next new trend. Ken has the mindset to figure out what the next new trend is. Sometimes he even creates a new trend, becoming the first to market with something that everyone else ends up copying. In New York, everyone always asked, "How did he think of that?" Ken often had me wondering the same thing! It's fun hanging with people like that.

Around this time, just after the crash, we joined forces to help people see the opportunities in commercial real estate investment and development through the maze of the market crash with its resulting upside-down values and opportunities.

In real estate, you must not only be creative, but you must also be able to weather cycles, maintain an ability to diversify into various markets, and be equipped with vertical integration to be the front runner. Over the years, Ken and I realized that our abilities were more complementary than competitive, and that we shared a goal. Despite the prosperous times that we all live in, most people do not retire financially secure. We realized it's time to catapult our 75 years of combined experience towards a worldwide effort, as detailed in the *Modern Wealth Building Formula*, to give opportunities to others through various real estate vehicles. Ken's formula improved his overall business effectiveness drastically, and it's the very strategies outlined in this book that we will deploy to grow and implement our new vision.

Today, I'm proud that Ken considers me a mentor who inspired him to reach this level, and I look at him as an awesome leader, trusted partner and true friend. This book is a gracious and honest revelation of the philosophy and strategy of one of New York's most successful real estate developers. It is not just an interesting read, but to the extent that you adopt some of the ideas that Ken shares, your own investing will be so much more successful.

I am a firm believer that "you never learn less". If investing in real estate is your game, then reading any book on the topic should serve you well, for if you spend $20 and three hours consuming the book, even just one idea may increase your cash flow by $10,000 a month. However, if the book also makes you smile, gives your cause to reflect, fills you with inspiration and motivates you to get out there and adopt some of its strategies, then you are on to a winner. This book does all of that and more.

Successful Investing!

Dr Dolf de Roos

Author of 15 books on real estate including the New York Times bestseller *Real Estate Riches*.

Ninety percent of all millionaires become so through real estate. More money has been made in real estate than in all industrial investments combined. The wise young man or wage earner of today invests his money in real estate.

Andrew Carnegie, *billionaire industrialist*

INTRODUCTION

Traditional Investing,

Traditional Problems

Since many of us were children, we were told about the value and importance of saving money. I still remember my mom, a teller at a small local bank, waking me up one Sunday morning before church as she put a piggy bank in my room. It was a ceramic replica of a Navy sailor with a huge duffel bag on his back. A small slit for coins and folded cash lined the top. While I loved the idea of putting my pennies in that sailor, what I didn't know was that Mom was simultaneously sharing the crucial power of the notion that a penny saved is a penny earned. Like most little boys, I would have preferred to spend my money on candy and baseball cards, but I eventually bought in and stuffed every dollar I could into that sailor to the point that the rubber gasket on the bottom busted out.

My parents taught me the little they knew about the wonderful world of banking, which made me fortunate. I will never forget the first time I set foot in our big local bank, walking out with a folded blue savings book with my first deposit stamped on the inside and a copy of my signature card with my new account number on it. It didn't offer the immediate gratification of folding dollars, with precision, to fit as many as possible into the piggy bank slot, but it was exhilarating to think I had my own bank account at the ripe age of eleven. It was a joint account, which my parents had access to as well. But I had them promise they wouldn't touch it without my permission. Over the years, my affinity for saving grew, and I eventually wondered what the heck I'd do with all the cash I had squirreled away.

I was pretty independent and loved doing my own research. Mom's older brother, Uncle Neil, was a vice president for a big Wall Street financial firm. We would meet in Brooklyn almost every Sunday for dinner at Grandma's railroad apartment. One week, he called me to say he had bought me a few shares of a hot stock. I didn't know what he was talking about, but I decided to find the answer. I read as much as I could about the stock market, and I absorbed a bunch of information about investing and the idea of buying shares of a business in hopes that it would outperform its current valuation. It felt cool to be a part owner of Coca-Cola, General Motors, and a whole bunch of other huge businesses throughout the United States. I guess you could call the stock market my gateway drug to investing. But as I learned more and more about various opportunities, I shifted my passion and focus to an entirely different investing mechanism: real estate.

Growing up in New Jersey offered an amazing opportunity to take field trips to the Big Apple. We thought of our teachers as rock stars when they scheduled those annual outings, especially since Hershey Park and Great Adventure would only keep our attention spans for a short time. I remember those New York City school trips as a young kid more than anything else. Many of my friends and chaperones wanted to tour the city, see the sites, visit Times Square, and eat some classic New York City pizza. But I just wanted to visit the tallest skyscrapers you could find. The construction, the architecture, and all the design that stood before my eyes fascinated me—that's how I felt as I stood for the first time on the observation deck of the Empire State Building. From my perch, I gazed over the New York City skyline in absolute awe of a buffet offering of this remarkable real estate, probably some of the best in the world. It started as an infatuation, but I eventually fell in love with real estate.

It got to the point where I wanted more than anything to find out how I could learn to develop real estate. The idea of taking a raw piece of land to create a magnificent environment with new construction and infrastructure—in short, a place you could call home—spurred me on.

I didn't know how or even where, but I knew I felt most comfortable among the giant brick and steel buildings on every New York City corner. And so, as much as I appreciated and still enjoyed following the stock market, eventually I replaced traditional investing with something much more exciting and lucrative: the real estate market.

In December 2017, *The College Investor* published an article that stated, "Over the last two centuries, about 90 percent of the world's millionaires have been created by investing in real estate. For the average investor, real estate offers the best way to develop significant wealth." Think about that for a second. Nine out of ten millionaires attribute their success and wealth to choosing property over the stock market. Pretty powerful stuff.

Investing in real estate produces consistent results with tangible assets that endure the weather of time. That's an important point to remember as we get started on this journey together. This book is dedicated to the life-changing investing strategies you can implement into your life. They will help you retire early and build astronomical wealth while minimizing the risk of traditional investment models. Now, I don't expect you to have all the necessary tools to hop right in, but I do hope that you will share with me an open mind in looking outside of the box and seeing what else is available to you and your overstuffed piggy bank.

Later in this book, I will introduce you to the Modern Wealth Building Formula, which will lay out in detail an investment plan that can change your life, provide you with a fulfilling journey in real estate, and ensure a pleasant retirement years before you had planned. But before we dive into any of that, let's first discuss why so many people choose the path of most resistance: traditional investing.

Traditional Investing

When it comes to traditional investing, individuals pursue investment return via two main vehicles: securities or real estate. You don't see normal everyday people pursuing mergers and acquisitions or even company takeovers. However, everyone on the planet wants a secure and honest way of having their money work for them. That's why they perceive that picking stocks or securities is the right path. They have been trained to think that way.

The traditional investment vehicles typically referred to in the textbooks include stocks, bonds, mutual funds, cash, and real estate. Each type of investment has its own advantages and disadvantages. All but one, in my opinion, require diversification. You've probably heard that before: You will lose if you don't diversify in your securitized investments. It would be crazy to invest 100 percent of your savings into just one company, even if it is a great one. Almost all forms of secured investments offered through fund managers require diversification because not all stock investments perform well at the same time. These different types of investments have opposite effects depending on world events, and changes in market rates and other economic factors can greatly impact them. So if you don't diversify your stock market investments and balance your portfolio, you will prevent your investments from sustaining the highest average return on investment.

Does that sound familiar? If you are a traditional investor in securities, then I bet it does. But that doesn't have to be the case. Maybe the coolest part about real estate is that there is natural diversification in each property. That might not make sense to you at first, but think about it like this: A single property is not readily reliant on one condition, environment, or factor. If you own a large apartment complex, losing one or two tenants won't make or break you. The fact that you have numerous filled apartments offers you the diversification you need to remain protected. Short of some serious act of God or catastrophic situation, you are naturally diversified in your properties. Unlike stocks, you don't have to buy more real estate to diversify your portfolio. Sure, it might make sense to buy some commercial and residential real estate and pick different areas of town, but that additional diversification can come as you grow.

Another concern of mine: In traditional investments in securities, you have no real control over the companies or securities in which you are investing. Life gets out of control at times, and strange things happen. Just look at a company like Enron. All it takes is a few bad apples for an entire portfolio—and company, for that matter—to get wiped out. With ordinary investments, you only get ordinary results. Or you get slammed by an unforeseen event, like a cyberbreach or the unexpected death of a CEO. Either way, I don't like the risk.

To that end, let's use layman's terms to look at the traditional investment options so that we can begin our comparison and presentation of the alternative strategies:

Cash: Invest your money in low-risk, short-term certificates or money markets.

Stocks: Invest your money in shares of stock for companies that you believe will increase in share value over a period of time.

Bonds: Bonds are a form of debt. Bonds are loans, or IOUs, but you serve as the bank. You loan your money to a company, a city, the government—and they promise to pay you back in full, with regular interest payments.

CDs: A certificate of deposit, or CD, is a type of savings account that has a fixed interest rate and fixed date of withdrawal, known as the maturity date. CDs also typically don't have monthly fees.

Mutual Funds: Invest your money into a pool of funds that are invested in securities that include a variety of companies diversified into different industries.

Hedge Funds: These are like mutual funds but with a pool capital from accredited and institutional investors that invest in much higher risk, higher reward, and more complex portfolios primarily for the advanced securities investors.

REIT: Real estate investment trust is a company with secured investments in income-producing properties in different sectors that range from warehouses, apartments, offices, shopping centers, and healthcare facilities, to name a few.

Other traditional securities are available to the common investor, but a combination of the just-referenced vehicles usually encompass most portfolios.

These are the traditional vehicles that require diversification as a MUST to reduce risk.

Why?

Because the stock market triggers valuation activity, and in most cases bonds and stocks move in opposite directions. When the economy reacts negatively, corporate profits typically drop and stock prices fall. When this occurs, interest rates may be adjusted to reduce borrowing and stimulate spending, which causes bond prices to rise. This type of diversified structure is typical for most securitized investors, which if diversified properly allows bond gains to offset stock losses to maintain a balanced portfolio. It makes sense and since you have no control, you must follow direction and be a good soldier.

My problem is that I like to be the captain. And I hope you will join me on this ship. If you are reading this book, you likely stand at a crossroads. You can further understand and gain expertise in the following strategies' traditional investment models, or you can unleash an entirely new approach to tangible real estate investments that reap much higher reward, less risk, and are much more controlled and fun. This modern approach can result in an incredible lifestyle and financial freedom. Sounds pretty good, doesn't it?

Traditional Problems

Research shows that more Americans than ever are retiring broke. This is a major problem that someone should address, don't you think? I've seen reports that show that higher than 40 percent of American retirees leave working life with less than $10,000 in their retirement savings. According to the US Government Accountability Office's 2016 data, Americans fifty-five and older have saved nothing for retirement. As we all know, Social Security cannot be relied upon for retirement income. CNBC.com, for instance, indicates that 65 percent of all Americans save little or nothing. It sounds like an epidemic to me; and maybe more important is the idea that we need to look at alternative investment options to address this epidemic.

From my experience, and for the lifetime of my stock portfolio, I believe we're up only 5.7 percent. That's because we have no control, we're not watching our portfolios every day, and we don't have time to figure out the game with nine gazillion companies lumped into mutual and index funds. We also don't have—or perhaps more accurately, make—time to become knowledgeable enough to dabble in hedge funds with higher reward and much higher risk, especially when we can't control our current security investments. Yes, I can keep reading books, but who has time to learn about the stock market when it is unlikely even in a best-case scenario to shift your returns above 20 percent? It just doesn't happen.

One of my friends owns and manages a billion-dollar hedge fund in high-risk commodities. He equips his trading team members with eight monitors at each of their desks, Bloomberg data feeds, and graphical data from various sources that you can't even imagine. After assisting in the development of the Lehman Mansion on Millionaires Row, his new corporate headquarters, he and I talked for just a few minutes about what drove him into what I perceived as mayhem. He was obviously very successful, and I wondered how the heck I might be able to successfully play that securities game too. The volume and speed of information is daunting. I've never really found anyone who has compelled me to invest in stocks, especially since real estate has worked so well for me. So does it make sense to just give your money to a broker and roll the dice? Or does it make more sense to participate in a movement to solve this epidemic and look at other investment options?

I'm speaking from experience in that I have participated in wealth mastery programs, set up systems to actively invest in securities, learned how to use stop losses, and played short and longs, puts and calls, and just about every other mechanism available to investors. But I was dizzy after setting up the systems and the process and worn out before I could even get rolling into the wild market. The amount of information you have to track leaves a normal investor in an impossible position to monitor and control his or her investments. They are at the mercy of others.

Eventually, security investing just wasn't for me, even though I'm pretty savvy with numbers. After thinking about it for a while, investing only in stocks, mutual funds, and securities is about as rewarding as losing a football game after playing hard for four quarters. So I recalled those trips to New York City and staring in awe at those amazingly beautiful skyscrapers. In doing so, I returned to one of my fondest memories and realized that real estate is the path to a happy life and successful retirement.

Now, I am not saying there is no place for securities and traditional investment. On the other hand, my wife was the breadwinner with securities. She saved a tremendous nest egg before retirement through securities and the company 401(k) plan leveraged though a major corporation and fund manager assigned to her corporate world. With her being the conservative one in our relationship, she achieved three patents in cosmetics and a large nest egg in case my plan didn't work.

In that scenario, employees have reputable selections of reliable secured investments with matching contributions. And you really don't have to do much in the process. Just stuff it away and let your limited results come to fruition. But that is not a viable plan for everyone. What do the people outside of major corporations do? Invest on their own? Hire a money manager? Those are about your only options, at least until you finish this book.

What does this all mean for you? Well, first off you should feel excited that you are about to unlock an entirely new opportunity to invest and save. Think about the potential impact on your future. If you don't at least consider the steps to address the traditional investing issues herein, you may become one of the retirement losers just discussed. The bottom-line problem is that most people retire with inadequate money to live the way they desire, and it leaves so many families stepping back after numerous years of hard work when in fact they should be stepping up into a better lifestyle when they retire.

In the Modern Wealth Building Formula, it's not about diversification. It's about calculated risk, cash flow, performance, and accountability. And for real estate, I have several opinions and approaches for you to consider.

Changing Your Approach to Change Your Life

Ninety percent—that is a powerful number. It supports the notion that if you want to swing for the fences and hit a home run, then real estate is your answer. Take a deep breath and ask yourself this: Do I want to use my good hard-earned money to live a great life? Do I want to retire with a level of freedom instead of being broke? If you answered in the affirmative to either of these questions, then WHY would you not get serious and take your current real estate activity to another level?

I am sure you can feel my passion for real estate. After more than 125,000 hours in real estate development and more than 100 deals, I must say that the tangible aspect to choose real estate investing was key for me. There is nothing like driving to the properties you own, being hands-on, walking through the commercial building you just acquired, touring the residential house recently built, and working to ensure that the property maintains stabilization and cash flow. These are all wonderful feelings.

Yes, it's like anything—real estate is a calculated risk, but it's a no-brainer compared to trying to learn how to control investing in the stock market. And what I'm sure about is that I don't want to earn typical returns that range from 3 to 8 percent on securitized investments when I can earn a minimum of 30 percent to a 450 percent return on real estate investments, get a quick hit of $100,000 to $250,000 occasionally, or have constant cash flow.

In the forthcoming pages, I'll also show you how a $1,000 investment can produce thousands of dollars in return. You will also undoubtedly love the syndication chapter when I show you how I developed a $17-million-dollar 72,000-square-foot ninety-unit, 113-bed assisted living facility with no money or experience at the time. The stories are crazy and invigorating and show just how wonderful real estate investing can be for all those involved.

We must create more believers who are committed to listening to suggestions. We must join hands and establish a structure for fulfillment so that ordinary individuals can establish investment platforms that benefit all. If most people continue to believe that they can't invest outside of their current means, we will remain stagnant. But if we can shift our paradigm and our minds to learn how to invest in real estate, then I can promise you that the sky will literally and figuratively be the limit.

Change can be frightening, and the temptation is often to resist it. But change almost always provides opportunities—to learn new things, to rethink tired processes, and to improve the way we work.

Klaus Schwab, *engineer and economist*

CHAPTER 1

RETHINKING YOUR APPROACH:
Why Real Estate? Why Now?

The old cliché "go with the flow" really doesn't apply when the tides are changing. When the flow is an undertow, going with it could lead to catastrophic consequences. So it should come as no surprise that the heartbeat of this book, and the point where we begin, is advising you to consider in what direction the "flow" has been trending in the past. We all maintain the ability to control our own destiny. So why not attempt to control your destiny and retire comfortably? In this chapter, I am going to offer you a new outlook on investing—a way to modernize the traditional approach. Together, we will shift your paradigm so that you can better understand and feel comfortable with the notion that sometimes you might drown if you just go with the flow.

The modern investing formula outlined in the forthcoming pages can reinvent the way you save for retirement, change your quality of life, and offer you a stress-free opportunity to build a strong foundation where your money works for you and not the other way around. Combining these elements of traditional investing, we have created the Modern Wealth Building Formula for real estate that is a viable option to secure financial freedom.

Changing Tides

As the tides rapidly turn, we need to reevaluate our investment system to better understand why people retire broke, even when they are doing all the right things leading up to their later years. The answer is that the only approach to investing in securities and stocks can actually set you up for failure. While you can look at the history of stock market crashes to see the ongoing trends and cycles, you better have an MBA and actuary license to fully understand the dire picture it paints. No matter what your broker tells you, he or she doesn't have a crystal ball and cannot predict the future.

Stock prices seem to be a mystery to even the most experienced investor. I never could establish the fundamentals from a layman's perspective for investing in the stock market. Have you? However, from my basic knowledge I understand that demand is the key factor in the price of a stock. While supply does change, its impact on stock price is very small relative to demand. Demand is defined as the amount of people and their money looking to invest in the market. Thus, the market cap (value) goes up and down based off of how much money consumers invest in the market. It sounds simple. However, what does this mean relative to your market investments? That's where things get complicated and Americans feel disengaged from their investments and savings. At times, there is just no rhyme or reason in the market. It is reactionary, but we aren't just what we react to.

Many people will tell you that the inequality of the market deters individuals because of the small percentage of people who control a high percentage of money in the market. According to a recent paper by New York University economist Edward N. Wolff, the top 10 percent of American households, as defined by total wealth, owned 84 percent of all stocks in 2016. CNN Business reported that "The richest 1% of families controlled a record-high 38.6% of the country's wealth in 2016, according to a Federal Reserve report." The numbers paint a stark picture of the inequality problems gripping the country. Not only that, according to the same CNN Business report, "The richest Americans are taking home an even bigger part of the nation's overall earnings." In 2016, the top 1 percent of families brought in a record-high 23.8 percent of the overall income. That's up from 20.3 percent in 2013 and about twice as high as the low point in 1992.

I asked myself this: What really makes a stockbroker any more qualified than the average educated citizen to make market recommendations when the people running the US Federal Reserve can't figure it out? In part, that is what pushed me to consider going against the flow and looking toward another option and opportunity. That is what led me to real estate. It's cut-and-dried—an acquisition price and then hard and soft costs determine total development cost. It's loan to value, equity required, projected revenue, and cash on cash on cash return. These seem much simpler than the numerous factors required to track a mutual fund with various companies, let alone the market and world conditions that affect US markets.

Playing the stock market is very similar to gambling. However, unlike gambling, the house is on the investor's side. Therefore, when stocks rise, the consumer and the company executives holding shares win. This opens a Pandora's box to a whole host of questions regarding a conflict of interest, insider trading, and trust. So if the stock market is such a great deal, why are more Americans not retiring rich? It could be the belief that all you need to do is find the right stock and hold on. Good luck finding it. Or it could be the cliché that you can't time the market, or that insiders have too many advantages over the rest of us and we don't have a chance. The bottom line is that people think the market is never wrong. That's a bit absurd. What if the market acts off of a false rumor? Do you want to lose all your money on gossip?

And if the market goes down when you pull your money out, guess what's about to occur for the next thirty years. It can all feel very cyclical. How will the extraction of money from the stock market affect your personal investment in it? Who really knows the answer? Seems riskier than real estate to me. Will they see the opportunity in real estate to stimulate the market, or will they contribute to another market adjustment? Your guess is as good as mine, and that's my point. Or could it be other factors such as limited returns, lack of knowledge, and/or lack of available savings that surgically extract us into a tizzy?

These preliminary factors scratch the surface of the issue. Other factors can be concerning. These additional factors may drive such an event of cash departure from the market that might impact the losses and limited returns on your investment in the long run. These include:

Tokenization. By now, you must have heard of the rise and fall of Bitcoin. You might even be wondering why this applies to real estate. Bitcoin is a type of digital currency in which a record of transactions is maintained. This digital transaction is the groundbreaking innovation of blockchain technology, which will cause drastic changes in almost every aspect of the financial world during any transition. I'm not so sure if it's predictable, fully beneficial, or a new cash machine for the feds once they regulate it in their favor. So what is tokenization? It's a catchall term that applies to every aspect of the blockchain industry and referred herein relative to tokenized securities.

Leaseum Partners recently announced a tokenized real estate fund using blockchain technology. This fund will issue shares as regulatory compliant security tokens listed on the exchange. That's interesting to say the least. What effect will this have on the securities and real estate market? For sure, it will throw Wall Street a new learning curve, or you may want to consider using tokenization and keep it as simple as possible to enhance your real estate portfolio when it reaches the everyday street.

There are questions as to what we might expect when we tokenize the world in the next generation with options like Bitcoin. For sure, it's a deep dive and requires in-depth analysis, but it's something that will obviously affect our personal investments. Tokens on a blockchain might eventually become the preferred mechanism for future money, shares in a company, or even a piece of real estate. There might be different types of tokens for different purposes. Payment tokens like Bitcoin could even be a payment gateway over the Internet. Utility tokens, analogous to an arcade token, will be used in exclusive blockchains. Finally, we might see a shift to asset-backed tokens representing real-world or digital assets, which can be comprised of real estate, personal property, and equity in businesses. The world is rapidly changing around us to include how we invest and pay for things.

The benefits may far outweigh the effects because of popularity, democratic wealth creation by making things available to everyone, enhanced security, cost effectiveness, and speed and global reach. Indicating this transition are major credit card giants like Visa and Mastercard, which have already adopted tokenization. Stay tuned!

Globalization. Globalization may have similar effects and has impacted nearly every aspect of modern life for the simple fact of the overwhelming number of goods we buy globally. Your personal investment can only be affected one way, and that's a loss in value. In theory, globalization provides a net benefit to individual economies around the world, and it's been mutually beneficial. The US stock market has had a much greater benefit over the last thirty years. This will change tide over the next thirty years because factors such as industrial growth, higher returns, and new, shiny opportunities elsewhere will attract many international investors into high-growth countries like China, South Africa, and India. This will cause millions of investors to pull out of the US.

Interest Rates. With current interest rates at an all-time low, the Federal Reserve will likely look to prompt inflation to get itself out of its massive debt. When interest rates eventually rise, projected earnings for most companies will fall and so will stocks. This typically results in losses within your portfolio. Without many options to recover, how does the Federal Reserve provide opportunities to investors? When people realize losses, I would suspect it would trigger the movement of funds into other investment options along with real estate..

Retirement. Currently, an enormous amount of retirement money is in the stock market through 401(k) retirement plans and pension plans, which comprise the largest groups of investors in public securities. This group often feels as if they don't have any options but the stock market. Baby boomers will take out most of their retirement savings over the next thirty years, sucking billions of investments right out of this traditional savings model. This will create continued volatility and instability in the market. In addition, as people age, you can hear the brokers screaming about asset allocation, diversification, and shifting away from equities as they get closer to retirement, causing a further step away from traditional savings models.

Taxes. There are current efforts to establish legislation that will allow people to invest capital gains in opportunity zones in the US, ultimately to defer those gains and eventually not to have to pay them at all if deferred for long enough. We all know that cutting taxes stimulates economic growth. However, since there is a massive limitation on our ability to lower rates any further, we don't really have this option available to us. More than likely, we will eventually see a rise in taxes on capital gains due to the climb in national debt, especially on high-net individuals who control most of the money in the market. If this happens, stock gains will look less favorable, which will be another good reason for people to rebalance their portfolio into real estate.

Workforce. If you are in finance, technology, or real estate, your future income and job security is probably tied directly to the stock market. So if you do invest in the stock market, the key to your success is riding it out, which will be difficult for the everyday American. It will be much more difficult to ride it out for the long haul if you are in a profession that's success is directly correlated to the stock market. You'll have extra income when the market is up, and you'll need income when the market is down. In this scenario, you won't have advantage of the long-term market trends and others will outgain you accordingly, leaving you ultimately with no control.

Technology. In today's world, public investors have less opportunities to invest early on in large technology companies like Facebook, Google, and Apple, all of which infuse money into the market through initial public offerings (IPOs). These companies have been successful with venture capital benefits to sustain the initial growth periods. In the dot-com boom, public investors capitalized and flocked to the market. However, since companies are now more sustainable than ever, they hold out and take on less money from capitalization.

The previous list is expansive but not complete. A number of additional reasons exist for why investors face challenging times ahead in the stock market. It is certainly not as safe and predictable as your broker would like for you to think. The issues just discussed should at least scratch the surface of the concern and outline why there are challenges should you continue to focus solely on investing in the market.

A number of other great opportunities are out there, and as I am sure you can tell, real estate is my preference.

Look Up, Not Out

Real estate is similar to nature in the sense that there is true beauty in the results. It reminds me of the passion my wife has as a master gardener. She's fascinated by the beauty of the numerous flowers she plants each year—perennials, annuals, raised beds, leprechaun villages, all the little particulars of her garden empire. This reminds me of my passion for all the skyscrapers in Manhattan and creating the beautiful landscape for Americans to learn, understand, and enjoy investing in properties. There is great beauty and unfettered excitement in real estate investing. It is tangible, present, real, and sensory.

Remember what Andrew Carnegie said about nine out of ten millionaires? It all started with real estate. With a statistic like this, it would make sense to look up, not out. Real estate is your true path to becoming a millionaire. For centuries, these types of indications have told us to essentially look up at the buildings around us and see opportunity to invest in each of them and to look at the wonderful beauty and exciting chance to enjoy a higher rate of return, a more tangible investment, and an immediate diversification.

Real estate has many advantages over investing in stocks, bonds, or mutual funds. It creates leverage and predictable cash flow, appreciates in value, provides a higher return, and increases your equity as you pay down your mortgage monthly. Let's unpack these at greater length so you can see why real estate is my investment of choice over the stock market.

Leverage. Leverage is the most important advantage in real estate investing! It increases your real estate value through the use of borrowed capital to increase the potential return of an investment. This also results in an increase to your personal net value.

How? The ratio of the mortgage loan to the value of your house is called loan to value (LTV) and typically dictates your leverage on a real estate investment. For example, if you take out a loan of $700,000 to purchase a $1-million house, the ratio is 700,000/1,000,000, which equals 70 percent. If the LTV is 70 percent, this means that for every dollar value of the property, the bank will loan you 70 cents. You have to come out of your pocket for the other thirty cents in the form of a down payment. In this case, for every thirty cents you can buy one dollar worth of real estate value, leveraging your deposit to buy much more value. Does that make sense? Now, if we add a couple of zeros, you can buy one million in real estate value for a $300,000 deposit based on an LTV of 70 percent.

So let's say that the property pays a 10 percent return on your investment per year on a $300,000 deposit investment. When you multiply 10 percent of $300,000, you would generate $30,000 per year in income based on the 70 percent LTV just described.

Now, to understand how leverage works, you need to persuade the bank to increase the LTV based on your track record and credit worthiness. In this new scenario you leverage this property to 85 percent, so you would only have to make a fifteen-cent deposit for every one dollar, instead of thirty cents. So, in the real estate transaction just described, you'd only have to make a $150,000 deposit. In this case, since the income stays the same and the deposit goes down, your rate of return on investment doubles. With a $30,000 income on a $150,000 investment, the rate of return is determined by dividing income over deposit—30,000/150,000. From this, you can see that the return of 20 percent doubles the rate of return with a higher loan to value.

Stability. The real estate market is usually much less volatile than the stock market, which creates more stability. Since it can take longer to liquidate your investments, this in turn increases a longer and safer period to significantly weather storms and market volatility. You cannot just pull out and reinvest like you might try to do in the stock market, which reduces emotional reactions and behavioral responses.

Tangibility. Real estate is ... well ... real. One of the main consideration factors for me is the tangibility of the real estate investment versus a stock investment. When using other people's money to create investment opportunities, there is nothing like what an investor feels when he or she conducts a virtual or live tour of a property, looking at it and/or touching it firsthand.

Easier to Learn. Investing in real estate requires much less education and training than the stock market. You do not need to know much about real estate to begin earning profits. On the other hand, the stock market requires a great deal of number crunching, accounting, and understanding market trends and history. It is research heavy, and you must be an active participate in it.

Easier to Start. You absolutely don't need to know everything about real estate or have any specialized knowledge to start investing in property. This is much different than the stock market. The beauty of real estate is that most of us will invest in at least one home in our lifetime. Given, we might live in it rather than treat it as an investment property, but we all mostly know the feeling—it is great to live in a home for a few years and then sell it for a profit.

Safer. There is a remarkable difference in risk between a stock investment and real estate investment. The risk in a stock market investment is measured by multiple factors in the corporate world, national and international events relative to profits and losses on investment, and a number of other factors that can change the value of a stock as quickly as the wind blows. Real estate is different in that it doesn't suffer these seemingly unexpected and immediate swings.

Predictable. Relatively speaking, real estate has predictable cash flow. All factors relative to cash flow are projected before your investment, with typical cash flow projection adjustment after one year of operations. In most cases, cash flow projections are within range and produce returns exceeding 20 percent.

Easy to Finance. Financing isn't available in a stock trade, especially when it's a hot stock and you want to leverage your bet. In today's world, hard money finance is very prevalent, very competitive, and easy to obtain in real estate. You can obtain nonrecourse money with low credit, where interest is paid at sale and interest loan rates are below 10 percent in many states. Based on the never-ending need for housing, permanent finance on residential properties is relatively easy as well.

Control. If you invest in the stock market, you typically need to hire a broker to handle your trades. Doing it on your own requires a full-time effort. This is much less the case in real estate. Once you close on the property, you own the asset and have complete control over it. That's a powerful statement, especially when you know that you can influence both value and cash flow.

Savings. Your hard-earned money and savings are basically placed into your house like a savings bank account. Most people purchase real estate with a small down payment and then typically pay the balance of the money owed by way of a mortgage. Over time, the principal amount of the mortgage is paid down. The reduction in principal is directly proportional to the increase in and building of your savings— your equity deposit—like a bank account. However, it is at a much greater rate of return.

Improvable. You can improve real estate and add value to your investments. Families do this all the time with kitchen and bath renovations, new siding and windows, or dressing up the landscaping. Whether the repairs are structural or cosmetic, do-it-yourself or hiring someone, the principle is the same: You can make your real estate worth more by improving it.

Price. Real estate prices range and vary by location. They are always negotiable to several terms, including the price. On the opposite side of the spectrum, in the stock market you are limited to buying shares at market rate at that time of purchase. There is no haggling.

Appreciates. One of the ongoing debates in real estate investing has been whether you should invest in real estate for cash flow or appreciation. US Census data shows that new homes increased in value by 5.4 percent annually from 1963 to 2008. Appreciation and tax structure are key factors to make deals work. My friend made millions of dollars in a real estate area with only a 2 percent rate of return on cash investment and a 20 percent forecasted appreciation. Even though there was limited cash flow, the increase in property value was quite impressive. Eureka!

Alignment. If managed correctly, real estate acts like a savings plan. You must put money down—called your "equity"—which is identical to putting money into a savings account. As you pay down the mortgage, the equity value goes up and you are essentially saving money every month by design, which aligns with every retirement plan.

Tax Benefits. You get the best of both worlds with deductions off properties such as capital expenditure, maintenance, improvements, and even the interest paid on the mortgage and personal expense benefits. These deductions and expense benefits offset income and reduce your overall taxes. This type of structure is the first step toward many advantages you will continue to have in real estate.

Depreciation. Depreciation is permitted in real estate and allows you to depreciate the value of your investment property over time. This benefits the investor because the value of your investment property actually appreciates. This depreciation benefit allows a real estate investor to generate more cash flow while reducing taxes. This results in a higher cash-on-cash rate of return than you may initially realize.

Lower Tax Rates. When investment properties are sold, the gains/proceeds are subject to capital gains tax rates. Depending upon your individual tax bracket, they are generally 15 percent or 20 percent. However, in securities, the proceeds are treated as ordinary income and taxed at the higher personal income tax bracket rates, whereas in real estate you have an additional tax advantage.

Deferrable. Under the 1031 Exchange regulation, our tax code permits the capital gain (profits) on the sale of an investment property to be transferred from the property being sold to a new property being purchased, deferring the payment of any tax on the sale of the property.

Flexibility. Depending on zoning regulations for the property you own, there may be options to subdivide it into two properties, where you can sell or develop the second property for a profit. While finding property for buy-and-hold acquisitions is relatively easy, finding properties with development options can require additional resources and be more challenging.

Easier to Hold. When the economy struggles, stocks typically go down and investors typically lose. But you can take a slightly different strategy in real estate. You are more prepared when and if all hell breaks loose. The property you own is always backup shelter and much easier to hold on to in troubled times. On the other hand, when a company falters, it's hard to hold on to stocks with losses. In real estate, provided you can make monthly payments, the bank is not going to call in the mortgage because of market shutters. And if the strategy works, you'll be able to continue holding your property until its value increases again.

Continued Growth. Choosing real estate as your primary investment strategy leads to continued financial growth after retirement. Following their corporate career, many investors have put together a nest egg for their retirement. There is great value in a combination of security-investment-paying dividends (income) and rental property to generate shortfalls. Whether its securities or real estate, your real estate portfolio value will continue to improve. This will make you worth more each year.

Keeping up with the Joneses. Real estate is a collective win, meaning that if your neighbors improve their land, then that increases the value of yours. As homeowners in the neighborhood perform home improvements, your property gets the benefits of their improvements. That's because the neighborhood has improved and therefore the value of the homes in the neighborhood increases.

As you can see, there are a number of viable reasons why real estate could and should be a preferred investment opportunity for you and your retirement. I am not saying there is no value in stock investments, but I am saying that there is a whole new world out there that you might not have considered. Real estate is a fundamentally easier process for almost everyone. In many ways, we have been trained to believe it is complicated and untouchable. But that is hardly the case. If you own a home, you're investing in real estate. It's easy to purchase, it's easy to finance, and there are no insurmountable financial barriers to entry. It's easy for most investors to improve their properties versus improving their stock values. And in the end, it has more tax advantages. While Wall Street is becoming more and more of a mystery to most Americans and becoming the game of financiers, real estate investing is looking better and better for the average American.

Ready, Set, Invest

So why not give it a try?

What do you have to lose?

Not much.

Surely, it's less than what you are probably losing in the stock market as of the writing of this book. In this chapter alone, you have navigated through very compelling reasons why you should take a step back from the market and toward investing in real estate. For most people, the stock market is kind of like a blanket ... warm, cozy, familiar. It is the way they've always done it. So you aren't to blame for being programmed to feel that the stock market might be the right fit for you and your retirement strategies. But just because something is warm and familiar doesn't necessarily mean it is the right path for you.

My goal is to help you get more comfortable with trading out your traditional, limiting investment strategies for a more powerful and safe mechanism. Over the years, real estate has offered me great opportunity and success. You can share in that journey. Throughout the rest of the book, we will continue to examine the tremendous value in real estate investing. We will also begin to help you build a foundation to start making small investments.

As you grow more comfortable with the concept of real estate investing, I will introduce the Modern Wealth Building Formula and then better illustrate how you can evaluate the market and obtain a competitive advantage over other investors. By the end of this book, you will be equipped with the knowledge to start your own real estate investment company and even turn your investments into a full-time business if you choose. The sky is the limit. As you leverage your efforts to create a revenue stream while also saving for retirement, I am confident that you will find yourself taking the elevator from the ground floor to the penthouse. So ... let's begin.

In the next chapter, we will discuss the Modern Matrix, which will help you better understand the different flavors of real estate investing out there.

The most difficult thing is the decision to act, the rest is merely tenacity. The fears are paper tigers. You can do anything you decide to do. You can act to change and control your life; and the procedure, the process is its own reward.

Amelia Earhart, *aviation pioneer*

CHAPTER 2

THE MODERN MATRIX:

The Different Flavors of

Real Estate Investing

In this chapter, I'll outline the preparation and mindset necessary to establish a custom Modern Matrix. Then, I'll outline the various flavors and opportunities offered in real estate investing. Finally, we'll dive into a proven strategy to ensure your real estate investing success. In following along, you'll develop an acuity for real estate investing.

The Modern Matrix

Let's first look at the Modern Matrix, a customized real estate approach and strategy for you, whether you are just getting started or want to take your portfolio to the next level. We will review a few customized Modern Matrix examples, how they apply to anyone (regardless of their favorite investment strategy), and how the matrix can save time and money, providing you have a strategy to devour real estate investing.

The Modern Matrix is not an array of numbers, symbols, or expressions arranged in *rows* and *columns*. Rather, it's an array of the types of real estate investing you have available to you as well as the levels in which you might want to participate in them. This matrix applies to any level of an investor, regardless of his or her experience, preferred level of participation, and/or target market sectors. Therefore, regardless of where you are in the process of real estate investing, this matrix is a ready-aim-fire approach.

The primary difference between the Modern Matrix and your old way of thinking is found in the process of real estate. In the traditional approach, you start at the bottom of the real estate pyramid with bird-dogging, then you move to wholesaling, fixing and flipping, and finally investing in a multiunit/commercial. Just like a dog trained to retrieve birds, bird-dogging in real estate is being trained to find deals. Most people start bird-dogging deals to make smaller amounts of money, like $1,000, $2,000, or $5,000. To that end, why wouldn't you bird-dog for larger deals that pay you $10,000 or $20,000? Society seems to tell us that you have to star at the bottom and work your way up to bigger and better opportunities. But the truth is, you have a choice: You can come out of the gate with my dynamic approach.

Now, wholesaling—also known as quick turns—and fixing and flipping are two areas of real estate investing you are likely most familiar with as they are the real estate buzz on the street (along with foreclosures, short sales, etc.). An insane number of competitors are clustered in flipping and wholesaling, as I know well from my previous experience as principal and CEO at Flipping USA. This red ocean saturation in residential is one reason I shifted toward writing this book to help people differentiate themselves, raise a $1-billion opportunity zone fund, and build more skyscrapers.

In wholesaling, you take control of a deal in the form of a contract—typically done for a few dollars—in which you assign the contract to another buyer for a higher price. You earn the spread in the prices, from contract price X to the quick-turn price Y on the assignment agreement. You'll often find a ready and willing buyer (many cases a fix and flipper), allowing you to make a quick profit with literally none of your money invested, if you choose. For example, on a wholesale deal, if you lock up and control a deal for the contract price of $125,000, and then a sell in a quick-turn assignment agreement for $152,000, you would earn $27,000 in profit. Now take a look at the return on your investment, as it's not something you want to share with everyone.

Assuming you locked up the deal for 10 percent of the contract price, that's $12,500. This ties up your money for a short period, only until the assignment buyer replaces your down payment with his money. Let me run you through the rate of return calculation, which Flipping USA did 137 times in 2016. Our average sale period was sixty-six days. Therefore, you would make a profit of $27,000 on your $12,500 investment. This is a simple process and explains why competition is fierce in the wholesaling arena. So how do you differentiate yourself to reduce competition?

Here's where it gets exciting. You can syndicate these small deals. The example below indicates the power of one of the subformulas we have in the Modern Wealth Building Formula. As the deals get bigger and take a little longer, the rate of return is relative. However, you can easily earn 10 x PLUS the profit margins. Take a look at the following table:

	YOUR $$$	INVESTOR
Period of Time (Days)	66	66
Contract Price	$125,000	$125,000
Initial Investment - 10%	$12,500	$12,500
Your $$$	$12,500	$1,000
Investor Equity	$0	$11,500
Assignment Cost	$152,000	$152,000
Your Profit	$27,000	$21,288
Investor Profit - 20%	0	$5,712
Annual ROI	216%	2,129%
Actual Rate of Return (ROI)	1,195%	11,773%
Investor Preferred - 15%	$0	$312
Total Investor Profit		$6,024
Annual ROI	n/a	50%
Actual Rate of Return	n/a	290%

The fix and flip model is one step above wholesaling on the food chain. Instead of selling your prize possession to a ready, willing, and able buyer, you fix and flip the property yourself. The "fix" may include anything from cosmetic landscaping to new siding, windows, and a roof, all the way through to a full interior renovation, with bathroom, kitchens, etc. remodeled—the whole enchilada. This approach takes a more intense strategy, but it's not difficult if you have a system. And remember, the margins are greater—especially if you get into the two to four families or if you follow my thought process and dive right into big-deal thinking or do what I did, fly just below the radar of the monster players and feed off the crumbs that fall. Your mindset must be informed by understanding the abundance that exists.

If we're honest, everyone's dream is to be a big-time real estate developer, owning numerous income-producing multifamilies, hitting the big leagues, and then retiring on an island—yippee! Well, it sounds great, and, trust me, it's rewarding; however, most people spend a lifetime to get there. I, too, spent a fair amount of time struggling. My lack of confidence, incorrect approach, limited resources and mentors, and minimalistic outlook all played a part. But, why not benefit from my hard knocks and start your real estate investing career at the top? Take these techniques and stop playing small. Step up to the highest level and survey the potential opportunities: residential, multiunit apartments, commercial office, retail on Madison Avenue, industrial parks, land development, and skyscrapers. Why set your target so low? If you ignore the larger targets, you'll plunge into retirement with no money.

Look at Sara Blakely, the self-made millionaire who founded Spanx. Before doing so she was a contestant on one of those daredevil reality shows. As a young woman with many career and financial challenges, she was competing against several muscular players, arguably more suited for the dare. The contestants were challenged with jumping off a cliff in an attempt to grab their dangling partner, and if they didn't grab on to the awaiting arms of their partners, they would plunge 500 feet into a ravine.

You can watch this video on YouTube. It's crazy! In the clip, the first contestant misses the target. It's frightening to watch and must have been maddening for those waiting their turn. The second woman leaps out and plunges in rotation twenty times. The intensity of the contestants standing in line to "walk the plank" is unbearable. The next contestant, a big guy who appears to have a shot, loses his grip on his partner's legs and down he goes. Then Sara steps up, and just before the big moment, she accelerates forward. You can feel her fly before she even takes off. As she magically leaps and nails her target, the small crowd of contestants screams in celebration. To see this accomplishment brings a tear to your eye when you think about the success or catastrophe that is all an arm's length away.

What was the difference between Sara's success and the failure of her competitors? At Grant Cardone's 10X Growth Conference, she recently told me that it was all based on her target. If you watch the video, the other contestants appear to be targeting the body of their dangling partner; thus, in each instance, they barely had a chance to grab their partner's legs. Sara said, "My target was the cable connection above her head, and that's the only reason I could hit the center of her body to hang on. In life, it's all about your target, aiming high and believing you can do it."

Her comment made me remember studying statics and dynamics at the New Jersey Institute of Technology. The first part of the course focused on statics, with various calculations on fixed objects. The second half dealt with dynamics, in which elements were moving—a more fascinating subject. So why would you want to be a static, fixed object? Why delay your success in real estate by taking an outdated linear approach? Why not employ a dynamic approach, using my proven strategies and results as a guide? Why not focus on a higher target, one that allows you to pass the competition and manage your real estate investments like an expert?

Why wouldn't you want to just *be*, *do*, and *have*?

As you choose your project types and market sectors and establish the investment structure you prefer, the Modern Matrix can act as an overarching navigation system customized for your journey. The matrix acts as your road map and plan of attack, informing your decisions and investments.

Below, I reference actual examples of the Modern Matrix for three types of investors: beginner, intermediate, and advanced. You'll see how their analysis sculpted a strategy for each of them.

Now, picture a line graph, where the *vertical axis* represents the participation level of the investor in ascending order: Bird Dog,

Wholesale, Fix and Flip, Buy and Hold, Renovation, Land Approval/ Sale, New Building, and Expert.

The *horizontal axis* represents the market sectors that investors can pursue based on market cycles and personal preference: Residential, Commercial, Retail, Industrial, Special Projects, and Skyscrapers/ Multiunit.

So, if you look at this as a matrix from where you see yourself now, where would you place a dot?

Are you a beginner, or maybe experienced in real estate, or possibly a bird dog for multiunits, or a fixer who wants to get into multifamily? Perhaps you are trying to get in with the big players in commercial, land development, and special projects. Take a minute to consider where you are now or may be shortly and where you want to go. If you are a beginner, you may need recommendations to get started. That's okay. No matter where you are in the process, you're in a perfect place to advance.

For example, draw an imaginary line from the vertical axis to the horizontal axis. Let's say you are in commercial and an expert. Put a dot where they intersect. Think through each market sector and level of participation and see what you discover. The ideas should flow, and your vision and paradigm for investing may shift. You have nothing to lose, so I would give it a shot!

Let's consider the matrix for client A in diagram one. This client specifically wanted to approach residential, and she was a beginner. Very committed, she wanted to become an expert in every area of residential, which included the gamut noted on the vertical axis. She also set specific goals for the initial step of bird-dogging. She would focus on bird-dogging commercial deals because her future hope was to be in commercial.

Diagram 1

MODERN MATRIX: CLIENT A

	Residential	Commercial	Retail	Industrial	Special Projects	Skyscraper
Expert	◉	◉				
New Building						
Land Approval/Sale	◉					
Renovations	◉					
Buy & Hold	◉					
Fix & Flip	◉					
Wholesale	◉					
Bird Dog	◉	◉				

Now look at client B, who had a different approach. Because he had experience, he was already involved in residential fixing and flipping. His goal was to secure buy-and-hold properties where he could start making passive income in addition to periodic profits over the duration of the year. This is a more consistent approach for retirement. Eventually, he could make $20,000 per month without pulling out of his driveway. And his long-term goal was to use his experience as a contractor to become an expert in commercial. During this process, he discovered a unique angle on special projects through his involvement in community groups, proving that the opportunities are sometimes right under your nose.

Diagram 2

MODERN MATRIX: CLIENT B

	Residential	Commercial	Retail	Industrial	Special Projects	Skyscraper
Expert	●	●				
New Building	●	●				
Land Approval/Sale	●					
Renovations						
Buy & Hold	●					●
Fix & Flip						
Wholesale						
Bird Dog	●	●			●	●

Now let's look at client C, an experienced overachiever who was an expert in both residential and commercial. He wanted to ratchet up operations across the board, utilizing his machine and systems to capitalize on new opportunities. After spending some time with me, he discovered an easy way to use this approach to help his children on their journey. He was already an expert, so this matrix became a snapshot that allowed him to visualize how to leverage his experience to help his children get started on their own path, not the path he may have wanted. He thanked me.

Take a closer look at the overachiever approach this client is taking. With his children interested in the business, this client expanded existing operations into retail and industrial, positioned his team for special projects, and even wants to give a skyscraper a stab. No fear with this cat.

Diagram 3

MODERN MATRIX: CLIENT C

	Residential	Commercial	Retail	Industrial	Special Projects	Skyscraper
Expert	◉	◉			◉	◉
New Building		◉		◉		
Land Approval/Sale	◉				◉	◉
Renovations	◉					
Buy & Hold		◉	◉			
Fix & Flip	◉					
Wholesale	◉		◉	◉		
Bird Dog	◉		◉		◉	◉

From the review of these client scenarios, and depending on your experience and investment goals, you can see how to create a real estate portfolio strategy that meets your comfort level while increasing flexibility and opportunity for you. For example, if you are a bird dog looking for small residential deals, it might make sense to keep your eyes wide open and look for bigger deals and outside-the-box opportunities along the way. Or you may be a residential contractor not fully using your potential to buy multiunit properties if you stay small and focus just on single-family deals. Or you may be an advanced investor who is across the matrix in all markets and active at all levels. The matrix may offer insight into a full-gear approach.

Using the Modern Matrix, you, the investor, can clarify your vision and develop experience-level acuity from day one. Traditional investors will lead you to believe that it could take five, ten, or even fifteen years to invest in anything but a fix-me-up. But that is not the case.

Flavors Aplenty

Most people who are active in real estate either buy passive-income-producing properties or lend hard money. But real estate investment opportunities remind me of an ice cream store with many flavors. If you were my child, I would tell you that to pick your favorite ice cream, you must try various flavors. If you don't try them all, you may never encounter the flavor you would like best. Real estate is often the same way but on a much greater scale. Any potential investment is a big decision, especially when you are going to be eating that flavor of ice cream for a long time. Real estate investing is similar, with many flavors to choose from. You may think you already know your flavor. However, I think it is necessary to outline all types of real estate investments you can consider as you apply the Modern Matrix.

In 2018, *Forbes* magazine noted that the value of residential homes in the United States is estimated at $31.2 trillion. That's a mind-boggling figure, right? It's more than 1.5 times the gross domestic product (GDP) of the United States and approaching three times the GDP of China. Residential value grew $1.95 trillion in 2018, with renters alone accounting for $485 billion. I find it hard to believe that people are not taking advantage of this golden opportunity, choosing instead to retire broke.

As we consider the flavors of your portfolio, you'll want to learn about the main real estate sectors you can choose from, depending upon your experience. For example, a nurse may be more interested in investing in a healthcare facility, like an assisted living or nursing home. A corporate executive may prefer an office building investment, or a truck driver may prefer an industrial investment. To each their own. Whatever you ultimately choose, you want to consider investing in a variety of opportunities, similar to diversifying a stock portfolio. And with the real estate market being cyclical, the savvy investor chooses to consider the Modern Wealth Building Formula so he can capitalize in any market cycle.

Generally speaking, four well-known types of real estate—and about a half-dozen risk factors—apply across the board. For our purpose, we will use the indicators Low, Medium, and High to scale risk level in real estate. Below are the well-known areas where most investors categorize their projects:

1. Residential
2. Commercial
3. Retail
4. Industrial

However, I like to break these categories down further. I want to expand your horizons and prevent you from thinking narrowly of only four opportunities when, in fact, many more are waiting. If I can open your eyes to all the possibilities, I can prepare you for the market cycles that fluctuate and compel real estate investors to jump from residential to commercial or industrial and back again as the different market sectors cycle and become hot again. If you are a serious investor continuously looking for opportunities, learning about many types of real estate deals will equip you with the knowledge to weather market cycles and increase your diversification. After all, it's important to have variety in both your life and portfolio. This multifaceted approach is, of course, based on your investment appetite and the criteria you established in your Modern Matrix process.

Residential Properties

Description: Single-family homes as primary residence, two-to-four-family investment homes, condominiums, co-ops, townhouses, duplexes, luxury and vacation homes

Risk Level: Low

Pros: Lower carry. After repair, the value typically exceeds cost to repair. You can also expect longer leases and fewer demands from a single tenant.

Cons: Single tenant, less diversified, homeowner fees, and maintenance costs. In the case of a primary residence, it's not an investment; it's your home.

Typical Investor: The typical investor is a single-family homeowner who watches his primary residence's property value increase. This experience wets his appetite, and then he may buy another property, typically another single-family home or perhaps a two-or-four-family home.

Commercial: Office Properties

Description: Typical commercial properties, as I define them, are corporate office, medical, and educational buildings. Other buildings, including multiunit residential, hotels, strip malls, restaurants, and convenience stores, may be defined as commercial for finance purposes.

Risk Level: Risk depends on factors such as type, location, class, tenant strength, and financial metrics. Commercial investment properties can be viewed in several ways relative to risk. Most people, including myself, use cap rate, which I believe to be a clear indicator of risk: the lower the cap rate, the lower the risk; the higher the cap rate, the higher the risk and the greater the reward.

Pros: Greater income potential with greater economic scale; income is passive; you catch the public eye; you are part of a bigger network, with triple net leases and limited hours of operations; it's also easy to obtain financing.

Cons: With a larger investment, one can expect higher risks; a single vacancy can be costly; professional help is required, and the time commitment, depending on your level of involvement (i.e., self-management) can be substantial; you're also vulnerable to downturns and higher maintenance costs.

Typical Investor: Seasoned

Commercial: Multiunit Residential Properties

Description: The popular multiunit residential property—think garden apartments, residential mid- and high-rise rentals—is often defined as commercial for financial purposes.

Risk Level: Low to medium

Pros: These properties produce larger, less risky cash flows, with a higher potential rate of return (ROI). In high demand, you'll feel less impact from sporadic vacancies and enjoy dollar cost averaging of fees and economic scale.

Cons: Multiunit properties can be costly and tougher to sell. You'll need professional help, so management fees will eat your profit. Potential headaches await, depending on your mindset. These properties are particularly vulnerable to a city downturn and require more secured financing based on tenant profile.

Typical Investor: Average buyers, private buyers, and institutional funds

Retail Properties

Description: Retail properties are exclusively used to market and sell consumer goods and services: strip and regional malls; single-tenant buildings that include big box centers (usually with national chains like Walmart and Home Depot); flagship stores on Madison Avenue; convenience stores; dry cleaners; bike shops; pharmacies; restaurants.

Risk Level: Low to medium

Pros: Retail properties can potentially yield higher profits, with a wider variety of investment types. They offer sizing flexibility, with multiple tenants and longer leases. Overall, they are typically low maintenance.

Cons: Directly related to the economy, these properties are quite sensitive. Changes in consumer patterns can be disastrous. Brick-and-mortar locations can close in this online economy. And you'll face larger investments with buildouts.

Typical Investor: I've noticed a diverse range of investors, including private buyers, international investors, and institutional investors.

Industrial Properties

Description: After the Recession of 2008, industrial properties have often been considered the most desirable class for the average investor because they require a smaller average investment, are less management intensive, and have lower operating costs. These properties include manufacturing buildings with large adjacent land tracts or warehouses, typically used for storage and distribution of goods. Other uses of industrial properties are research and development, manufacturing, TV studios, and climate-controlled storage.

Risk Level: Low

Pros: Benefits can be seen in the stable and predictable cash flow, attributed to ecommerce; less expensive to own and operate; longer lease terms; fewer landlord responsibilities; and variety.

Cons: You are dealing with specialized tenants—a single tenant in many cases. With less availability, you'll wait longer for rewards, and this niche is definitely not glamorous like skyscrapers.

Typical Investor: Investor with low-risk tolerance and stability who looks at long-term gain for retirement

Hospitality Properties

Description: Hospitality consists of properties that provide accommodations, dining, and other services for travelers. This is primarily known as the hotel sector and includes casinos and resorts. You may have stayed at a flagship hotel, like a Marriott or Hilton, or at boutique hotels located in most major cities. With tourism, the hospitality sector is the largest growing industry and remains afloat during hard times.

Why?

A hotel industry analysis reveals that bookings in travel and tourism hit almost $1.6 trillion in 2017 and that travel and tourism now accounts for over 10 percent of the global GDP, thanks to a strong global economy. According to industry statistics, the total revenue of the hotel industry in the USA alone should exceed $200 billion in 2019. It's a sector you want to keep an eye on.

Risk Level: Risk varies based on the type of hospitality (asset class): limited services (low), extended stay (medium), and full-service luxury resorts (high).

Pros: Short-term fluctuation and interest rates do not normally impact this type of investment.

Cons: Life cycle, development risk, operating risk, and exit strategy limitations

Typical Investor: Accredited and sophisticated investors are drawn to this sector.

Healthcare Facilities

Description: Healthcare includes acute care hospitals, ambulatory surgery centers, cancer centers, cardiac care treatment centers, emergency centers, hospice, long-term care facilities, medical laboratories, medical office buildings, rehabilitation centers, respite care homes, and specialty facilities.

Risk Level: High

Pros: Attractive, specialized needs, market cap

Cons: Investors in this sector must be informed about current regulations for such facilities. Other cons include subsectors without long-term growth plans and inappropriate supply sources.

Typical Investor: Investors associated with healthcare, accredited

Land

Description: These properties include vacant land, working farms, and ranches.

Risk Level: Medium to high, depending on your exit strategy

Pros: I see a big upside for the investor who knows how to navigate entitlement and approvals. The savvy investor can sell approvals for substantial profit and can also, if capable, develop the property for even large profits and continuous passive income.

Cons: High risk, high reward, and minimal margin for error as builder and developer

Typical Investor: The typical investor is seasoned and well versed in entitlement, most likely with a minor technical background with a big target on earning fees through the approval process, awaiting the big windfall at the exit strategy, i.e., sell approvals or fully develop.

Data Centers

Description: This category includes an array of storage and transfer facilities, including data centers, call centers, and trading floors. This is one of my specialties from projects at MetroTech in Brooklyn and Prudential Securities at One New York Plaza. As technology grows, and with the introduction of the cloud, the majority of data will move into cyberspace; however, millions of square feet of real estate for data storage will still be required.

Risk Level: Medium

Pros: As data increases, more demand for controlled storage space will occur.

Cons: You need technical savvy to understand the intricacies of data centers and all additional requirements, such as redundant and back-up systems, which have high operating costs. If new construction, this type of project takes longer to build than structures for other sectors.

Typical Investor: Experienced and accredited

Portable Dwellings

Description: Affordable housing for low-wage earners, such as mobile home parks and the new fad, tiny houses

Risk Level: Low

Pros: With less competition, less capital, steady demand, lower turnover, and low maintenance, this type of property has a high upside for the investor.

Cons: With lack of financing, depreciation, and low-wage clientele, you'll see low to moderate return unless you are the developer.

Typical Investor: Individuals with high net worth and private buyers

Mixed-Use

Description: The result of combining any of the above categories
Risk Level: Medium to high
Pros: Larger developments like The Villages in Florida, or one-stop shops with multiple income streams, command premium rent if there are amenities, additional tax benefits, and promotion of social interaction and attraction
Cons: Financing is more difficult as uses are evaluated separately, with different interests and goals among residents versus commercial owners. You can face limited retail profit due to limited foot traffic in a rural area.
Typical Investor: Savvy, experienced, accredited

Special Purpose Projects

Description: Special purpose properties include churches, self-storage facilities, amusement parks, golf ranges, golf courses, water parks, ice rinks, athletic facilities, and bowling alleys. Consider your social circles; you may be surprised at the opportunities under your nose.
Risk Level: High
Pros: With great entitlement play, these projects are quite market-able in populated areas. Niche markets are exciting as they produce high profits. But don't get emotionally attached to the glamour; make sure the numbers are vetted, please.
Cons: These properties may be seasonal or specialized, requiring long hours of operation. There may be long-term entitlements, lengthy with opposition, and economic spending.
Typical Investor: Savvy, experienced, accredited
As you can see, a number of different flavors are available in the real estate ice cream shop. Some might be for you and some might not. That is the beauty of opportunity: It comes in many shapes and sizes. As we move through this book, you'll get a better understanding of each investment mechanism, enabling you to choose the right one for you.

Getting Your Feet Wet

At this point, you may be wondering how you will develop a strategy to break free from employment or help you put your hard-earned extra money to work for you. Or, like I was, you may simply be tired of not being able to control your stock portfolio. You may be a beginner or a current stock investor who is ready to try something new. Or you may be ready to retire and in need of a place to put your 401(k) to work. In all of these instances, the common thread is seeking tangible assets for higher returns. Real estate investing is a phenomenal option after retirement instead of diversifying a portfolio into less risky bonds with lower returns.

Let's take a few minutes to look at strategy. To fully put the matrix to work, you have to first consider the role real estate plays in your investment portfolio. I have two-thirds of my portfolio in real estate, and it works for my family. It has given us more control and a much bigger upside. I would recommend this approach to everyone. Two-thirds of my portfolio is diversified in residential, commercial, and special projects. This selection of market sectors creates another layer of diversification, which keeps me safe and sound and may initiate an inquiry about strategy.

My Google search for "definition of strategy" resulted in strategy as a *plan of action or policy designed to achieve a major or overall aim*. Let's break this down. A plan of action alone has dozens of items, many relatively simple. However, you have to assess the tasks and then put those tasks into compartments to exponentially increase your chance of achieving your outcome. You must also determine the items you can assign versus the items only you can execute.

Planning is the first step for any real estate investor. I use the Rapid Planning Method, which is Tony Robbins's RPM system for planning. He uses this system to run dozens of companies and even to run his life. I've studied both his project plan for Robbins Research International and his personal life plan. His method is a reverse of traditional thinking in which you start by defining the desired end results; then you clarify the purpose; then you create a task list to establish duration, priority, and delegations, which should streamline your plan. With reverse engineering, the optimal order for success is outcome, purpose, and then task. This allows you to discern the 20 percent of tasks that, if conducted, will allow you to obtain 80 percent of the results you desire.

Now let's look at this strategy from another perspective. To build on the Robbins approach, I've parlayed the Blue Ocean Strategy and applied it to my real estate venture and educational programs. Here the investor compares blue ocean strategies with red ocean strategies.

Red oceans represent all the industries in existence today—the known market space. In the red oceans, industry boundaries are defined and the competitive rules of the game are known. Here companies try to outperform their rivals to grab a greater share of product or service demand. As the market space gets crowded, prospects for profits and growth are reduced. Products become commodities or niche, and cutthroat competition turns the ocean bloody, hence, the term "red oceans."[1]

Blue oceans, in contrast, denote all the industries not in existence today—the unknown market space, untainted by competition. In blue oceans, demand is created rather than fought over; ample opportunity for profitable and rapid growth exists. In blue oceans, competition is irrelevant because the rules of the game are waiting to be set. Blue ocean is an analogy to describe the wider, deeper potential of market space not yet explored.

In essence, red represents blood from the competition of saturated markets while blue represents peace and no competition.

Whatever approach you decide to take, you have to strategize as you mix and match your choices for market sectors, investment types, and the roles you want to play. If you are serious about making money, then you, of course, want to obtain financial knowledge and real investment guidance to ensure success. With that said, I hope you are collecting the variables for your Modern Wealth Building Formula so you can understand the differences between residential and commercial real estate investing.

The purpose of the Modern Wealth Building Formula is to help you move from the old way—financially bound and working for an employer with limited time to do what you want—to the modern way, in which you are financially free to do what you want, when you want, however you want. To achieve this move, you have to acknowledge three old beliefs and make three essential mind shifts, allowing a paradigm shift to occur. This is required along with the elevator to the penthouse process that includes the Modern Matrix.

And that is the topic of the next chapter.

Opportunity is missed by most people because it is dressed in overalls and looks like work.

Thomas Edison, *inventor*

CHAPTER 3

THE MODERN WEALTH
BUILDING FORMULA:
FIND, FUND, FACILITATE

This haunted me: a CNBC report that stated about 42 percent of Americans have less than $10,000 saved, according to a study by GoBankingRates, and knowing the difficulties our new generation faces just to get their feet on the ground. I wanted to solve this societal problem. I knew I could help others use real estate investing as a powerful form of saving, investing, and increasing cash flow to do just that. This led me to create the Modern Wealth Building Formula, the topic of this chapter.

I derived the formula from my life in real estate and found a direct application to business professionals that trade time for money and want their hard-earned dollars working better for them. It's for the professional practitioners that include dentists, doctors, lawyers, engineers, and architects, just to name a few. It also applies to employees that want to break free from the constraints of simply cashing a paycheck. Since I didn't want to be one of those unfortunate investors or retirees, I created a formula that shifts your mindset and then sets you up to implement a powerful SYSTEM to Save Your Self Time, Energy, and Money so that you can create passive income for retirement, security, and peace of mind.

Here's the good news: You don't need your own money. You don't need vast experience in real estate. You don't even need a specific formula for your demographics or current career. Years ago, I was a civil engineer designing development sites in New Jersey, and now I'm a successful national real estate investor. Trust me, such a transition can be much easier if you're willing to learn and use the Modern Wealth Building Formula.

What you need is a commitment to make changes to look at what you don't know. You need to be willing to reinvent yourself if necessary. You need to be dedicated to obtaining mentorship so that you can learn new skill sets quickly rather than spending time spinning your wheels trying to manage the unknown. The actions on your commitment and dedication will then dictate your choices so that you can get in the game or take your game to the next level. Essentially, if you are committed, we can teach you the skills and steps to move forward.

The Discovery

Before we dive into these steps, I want to share with you how I created the Modern Wealth Building Formula. A couple of years back, I realized that building an extraordinary life is just like building skyscrapers (which I had done) in New York City. As I further developed this simile, I focused on variable success principles, developing a formula that worked and then delivering impeccable real estate outcomes on time and under budget. Doing so has been one of my main motivators for a good part of my life. This led me to consider how I overcame challenges and stoppages in my own life and career and how I eliminated the fears that caused me to freeze in my tracks. I then turned my attention to the many traits I utilized and how I could transform the traits into a formula that could help others.

As I looked deeper into skills that helped me succeed in the major leagues of real estate, I came up with four very important personal qualities: massive effective actions, a habit learned from my Tony Robbins life mastery training; wisdom from over 125,000 hours of dedicated service in real estate development and construction; bold leadership attained from world-renowned mentors; and forward outside the box thinking.

As I wrote down those four qualities, a word puzzle formed in my mind. I extracted the first four initials of each statement—M W B F—and started to daydream around them. It was within a split second of thought that the **M**odern **W**ealth **B**uilding **F**ormula came to life.

I saw a distinct complementary alignment between the Modern Wealth Building Formula and two primary components that I am about to describe that enabled me to master the real estate investment process. It was an opportunity for me to start a new chapter in my life and work toward fulfilling my refined purpose, which is to use my drive, tenacity, and knowledge in real estate to inspire, motivate, and assist people in reaching their goals in real estate and in life.

With all that said, let's break down this formula. The Modern Wealth Building Formula was derived by the following traits:

MWBF = M + W + B + F

M = Massive Effective Action

W = Wisdom

B = Bold Leadership

F = Forward Outside the Box Thinking

There are two primary components of the Modern Wealth Building Formula:

1. Shifting your mindset (various paradigms) related to real estate investing

2. Implementing the three-step formula that I am about to outline

Let's unpack each of these primary components at greater length and why they are essential for the FIND, FUND, and FACILITATE process, which are the three phases of real estate investing and the key to the Modern Wealth Building Formula working most effectively.

Shifting Your Paradigm

Your mindset, or paradigm, is more than half the battle when you are either building your own real estate empire or fighting for your economic well-being, be it retirement or getting out of debt. So what is a paradigm shift? The dictionary defines it as a fundamental change in an individual's or society's view of how things work in the world. In other words, it's how the world occurs to you or how you have created a model of the world that dictates your belief regarding the world. Paradigms control you and your future. A paradigm is a belief ingrained in your subconscious that can unconsciously stop you from achieving what you want. It can even cost you happiness because it literally controls the results in almost every aspect of real estate and life.

Your paradigm controls your perception and your logic. It controls how you use your time, and it controls how you make money. Therefore, if you want to change your life, or your future, you MUST change your various paradigms and overall mindset.

Ask yourself, "Can I turn my annual salary into a monthly salary?" If your first instinct is to say "yes" or "no," that instinctive language pattern will lead to your belief system. And what you believe can very well come true with a certain paradigm. As Einstein said, "If you believe you can or can't, you are right." Think about how many times your mindset has either hurt you or helped you. The truth is that your paradigm is either the key to unlock your treasure chest or not.

To dismantle the paradigm that may be holding you back, you need to understand that a multitude of thought habits are programmed into your subconscious and only you can change these thoughts, habits, and/or beliefs through repetition of your vision and affirmations, a series of language patterns that will reprogram your subconscious.

Therefore, you must consciously select new beliefs and in turn choose new habits aligned with your new beliefs and goals, followed by structured repetition, as noted, to break the ineffective patterns. Otherwise, you will form just another set of bad habits instead of taking advantage of being a creature of habit moving toward a great habit to practice the Modern Wealth Building Formula.

Three ways of thinking often stand in the way of our progress in real estate investing:

You need lots of money to invest.

You need experience to invest.

Your geographical location has restrictions.

If you don't believe me, please trust from my experience that these are the most likely obstacles stopping you. But the truth is that they are all in your head. They simply aren't real concerns and only thoughts you've made true. We have disproved them time and time again. Now let's examine the three mental shifts.

First Paradigm Shift: You don't need lots of money to invest.

I had no extra money available when I started thinking about real estate. I was twenty-nine and lucky to have a job and the ability to barely pay my monthly bills. My credit card debt was eating up any extra money to even fathom being a real estate investor. I was more worried about whether I could afford a vacation on my time off. It was not until I discovered syndication that it could ever have been imagined that I could be in real estate.

Once I realized that all I had to do was put a deal together, I thought about the movie *Field of Dreams*. We've all heard the famous line inspired by that movie: "If you build it, they will come." Applying that to my life, I knew if I could only build an investment package, the investors would come. Sure enough, I found a twelve-acre property with an approval to build an assisted living facility on it. I locked up the deal, and I was off and running broke with no experience. Using the methods outlined in this chapter, I figured it out and completed the project in twelve months.

Second Paradigm Shift: You don't need experience to invest.

At thirty, I cut the ribbon on a $17 million 72,000-square-foot, 90-unit assisted living facility with no real estate investment or development experience. How? By surrounding myself with people who know more than I do. They guided me through the process. I found an architect that had done it before. He brought in his team, and the township attorney directed me to the planner and engineer. I then solicited several general contracting bids so I could learn every cost. Suddenly, we were on the field with a team in place.

The good news is that you can be guided through the process on any real estate project. The trick is in recognizing how not to lose money during the process. That took me many more years to achieve. Now my participation in development projects acts as an insurance policy because of my ability to prevent pitfalls and losses. After figuring out how to complete a $17 million project on time and under budget, I had just enough experience to be dangerous, quickly improved from my mistakes, and went on to rinse and repeat this process.

Third Paradigm Shift: Your geographical location does not impact the formula.

Many people believe that real estate investments don't exist outside major cities. Or they claim that their opportunities are limited in certain areas of the United States, specifically in rural or depressed neighborhoods. But this just isn't true. The housing market alone ($31.2 trillion) offers real investment opportunities in every city and state. That is 1.5 times the annual 2018 US gross domestic product, so I'm not buying into this notion that geography makes a difference. There are also many commercial and real estate development investments under your nose. Once you Awaken the Giant Within—thank you Tony Robbins— you'll realize and take advantage of the opportunities.

We investigated the formula on residential and healthcare living alternatives for the mentally disabled in North Carolina, which gave us the opportunity to try our formula outside of our typical demographics on residential and commercial properties. The healthcare plan was difficult to manage in North Carolina due to the lack of local qualified people in position. After stepping back to some basics to establish and create a presence in multiple areas, we were off and running, able to establish ourselves as qualified investors. We have since shared the formula with many clients who have used it successfully in Illinois, Pennsylvania, Texas, Delaware, New York, New Jersey, Connecticut, Rhode Island, California, Arizona, and Florida, to name a few places, with raving results across the board. It was then we realized that the approach works everywhere.

The three paradigm "obstacles" just outlined often stand in the way of great progress and opportunity. But the truth is that they are all in your head. They simply aren't real concerns. We have disproved them time and time again. Once you shift your mindset and feel empowered to invest, you are ready to move into the second part of this process, a powerful formula that can change your economic environment. There are three areas of expertise in the second part of the Modern Wealth Building Formula: Find, Fund, and Facilitate.

For the remainder of this chapter, we will unpack each of these areas at greater length.

The First Step: FIND

The first step to find profitable deals effortlessly includes a bit of pregame conditioning or preparation, just like any sport. There is a preseason to get you warmed up and in shape to prevent injury and prepared for the season opener. Similarly in real estate, you need preparation and structure for fulfillment, a reversed engineered plan to be effective and prevent losses.

The Three Step Pregame Formula

Once you've shifted your mindset, you clear space for additional mind capacity to create exactly what you want. This pregame warm-up prepares you for the mindset acuity exercise and your path to find profitable deals. This is the key to clearing your mind and then blasting your mindset with new acuity, to see things you've not seen before, which leads you directly into the investment goals and criteria exercises.

These three exercises include:
1. Mindset Sensory Acuity Exercise
2. Investment Goals Exercise
3. Investment Criteria Exercise

These three steps in the formula are for a specific reason as you proceed into using our approach to Find, Fund, and Facilitate. They are

43

recommended as pregame and preparation exercises toward the first step, FIND, because the first step in any successful investment strategy is FINDING the right investment for your portfolio. The same is true in real estate. Thus, you are likely wondering about the answers to important questions like:

How can I get started and find my first deal?

How do I scale my existing properties into a full-time real estate business?

These are both normal sentiments and concerns. The point is you have to explore both as they may apply if you're already investing and going for a bigger deal. It also may depend on your comfort level to assess the variety of options available to formulate the right plan of action that will attract investors. It can vary from investor to investor. No two people are the same. But to kick things off, bring it on toward FINDING the right investment for you. Because without your mental clarity on what you are specifically looking for, you have no ultimate leverage when you and the universe are confused, which leaves your target a crapshoot.

These three exercises result in the clarity and leverage to find the right investment for you in addition to attracting the right investors to support your investment goals.

Let's discuss each at greater length.

Mindset Sensory Acuity. The mindset acuity exercise is part of my method to further shift your paradigm so that you can create your own new vision. As we already know, maintaining a positive and/or a strategic mindset is half the battle in anything we do. As you begin looking for an investment, always digress for a minute and look at the big and the long-term picture. Do you have a plan? What are your exit strategies? How much money do you need to execute the next step? Be real and authentic. It's perfectly fine to work on clarity, which assists with leverage because you are formulating a plan. However, without identifying effective actions with which to move forward, it will be difficult to determine exactly where you want to go.

You can reference the Mindset Acuity Map at https://resources. kenvanliew.com/Mindmap.pdf so you can enhance your sensory acuity around real estate. You may already be in the game. So if you want to learn something new, look at this mind map from the perspective of having a clean slate—in other words, what you don't know, you don't know. The mind map gives you a snapshot of a series of investment and development categories and how they integrate amongst each other. This is not something that happens overnight. Rome wasn't built in a day and this is not a get rich scheme, but it is the fastest track to wealth. This mind map is a meticulous analysis of the mindset acuity you need to succeed in big-time real estate.

Do you remember when you started driving with that new freedom? Driving for the first time gave me an entirely new kind of acuity. I remember the first day on the road in 1979. I saw a Trans Am for the first time and then the next week I saw many and all my new favorite cars; it was like a handful of shiny pennies. Driving offered me the big picture. The same is true in real estate. If you are going to make a deal, you first need to have an understanding of all these mind map components. And you want a perspective that will help you talk intelligently to investors about the "who, what, where, and why" of your plan.

Investment Goals Exercise. Once you are clear about your vision, goals, and target market, you will quickly find an absurd deal flow if you have not planned accordingly to filter profitable deals. The criteria filter is the key to success in finding profitable deals that meet your investment criteria. Establishing criteria is similar to preparing for a target, where you get ready, aim, and shoot—it will save you huge amounts of time and money over the course of any deal. Who has time to waste anyway?

How do you get profitable deals brought your way? You start to accomplish this with expanded sensory acuity and clarity of your goals with an investment target. This allows you to establish your investment criteria and then demonstrate and teach your network and dream team about what you want in your deals. With this approach, you kill two birds with one stone. You can then establish your deal flow system with profitability projections and my recommendation to complete an Investment Criteria Exercise similar to one in our online curriculum.

Investment Criteria Exercise. This may not be in the context of your initial thought, and it's different than criteria you may want as your preferred rate of return on a personal investment. This is about the investment criteria required to syndicate a deal where you use investors' money to fund your deal. You must be able to talk intelligently about the criteria to your investors without sticking your foot in your mouth and blowing the deal.

In one instance, you want to tell people what you're doing in hopes of eventually talking serious business, getting a sweet deal, or closing a big investor. To start presenting what you are up to in your newfound investment strategy, clearly establish your investment criteria to go big or go home. This follows the Sara Blakely high-target approach mentioned earlier to ascend in lieu of falling short with nothing, which resulted in her becoming a billionaire.

If you're raising funds from investors, you will eventually get fired upon with questions; and if you want to step up into real estate, you will not be able to avoid stepping out of your comfort zone and possible confrontation. What type of deals are you proposing? This would be another way of asking: What are the investment criteria? Therefore, you probably have realized by now that the criteria are the components of the investment. For example, we provide investment opportunities in the tristate area, targeted at one to four families in both wholesale and retail residential investment markets that range from $100,000 to $750,000 leveraged at 75 percent LTV (Loan to Value). You have to say something ...

It may continue like this. These investments have equity positions that range from $50,000 to $250,000 that pay out to our investors an annual ROI (Return On Investment) in the range of 8 to 12 percent. In the event we find properties highly recommended to buy and hold, we target lower cap rates with an upside from building or property improvements to entitle raising rents, net operating income, and property value.

This example gives you the investment criteria in a nutshell when you are speaking about your investment strategy and deal criteria. You are a walking, talking dealmaker. You hit upon the primary data points an investor wants to hear in one swoop. You can't beat around the bush in your presentation. It's like *Shark Tank*. Short and sweet, hit them between the eyes, and then follow up with the paperwork. It's a one-two punch.

The pump is now primed to FUND profitable deals.

The Second Step: FUND

Funding is a process. It's not only about the end game of collecting the money. It's serious and incorporates meeting obligations as well because your success is where this internal preparation meets opportunity, and the preparation is necessary to position yourself to raise big money. Funding can also be defined as leveraging your own money in real estate to acquire property or invest in a project. Additionally, it is a term used for the capital stack needed to support larger projects. It can also be synonymous with financing, with reference to capital stack of monies including various types of funds that comprise the entire finance package called capital stack.

The capital stack (the stack of money you need to buy the real estate) generally used as reference to funds on larger projects typically includes four forms of interest in your real estate investments. Typically, it also includes two forms of equity that include common equity and preferred equity and two forms of debt, which are mezzanine debt and senior debt.

The funding process includes a few variables as noted, the most common being equity and debt. If you want to raise funds, be familiar with both of these. Fundraising is the primary role in the real estate investment process because if you don't grease the wheel and fund the investment, your journey will have serious challenges.

Let's look closer at the steps you need to take to get your financial feasibility in order and what's required to take your presentation skills to the next level so you can shatter your goal. With this approach, as Stephen R. Covey says in similar words in Habit 7 of *The 7 Habits of Highly Successful People*, you will need to "sharpen the saw." In other words, sharpen the saw (sharpen your skills) so that you reduce the required work to succeed or cut down many trees.

Another MUST is one of my favorites, Jack Canfield's *New York*

Times bestseller *The Success Principles, 10th Anniversary Edition*. In Principal 34, "Develop Four New Success Habits a Year," you can only imagine that in five years you could develop twenty success habits that could bring you all the money you want.

During the funding of any project, your presentation will make or break you. Carefully prepare your presentation so that you can obtain the funds necessary to execute your plan. The bulleted/highlighted actions in the Fund step that follows are highly recommended if you want to get into the real estate game with a thriving plan to raise funds that will allow you to accomplish your goals.

Based on the significance that money plays in real estate investment, you should prepare your presentation for the numerous opportunities that will be presented to you. Look at this as a double-sided coin. You can't lose if you understand that the level at which you present is directly proportional to the amount of money you raise and opportunities that will come your way. So it's critical that you follow this thought process and approach to move forward as I did and then the floodgates will open with the flow of unlimited funds.

Now, I suggest that my top-down thinking here applies across the real estate investment gamut. It especially applies for raising funds, which starts with a detailed plan and presentation at the highest level to maximize the facilitation of the investment process, the next step in the Modern Wealth Building Formula after we complete this most important section on the funding presentation.

Here are the three important pieces in any great FUND presentation:

- **Investor's Business Plan.** My approach is a little different in the sense that we help you create your own modern investor's business plan versus a traditional business plan. We prefer this format because it's written from the perspective of the investor—what's in it for me? The investor's business plan is our biggest confidence builder because it establishes where you are and where you want to be. Then it allows you to fill the gaps and ultimately create extraordinary presentation material. It can then be streamlined into a one-sheet advertising piece, website content, marketing leave-behind, or a full-blown investor business plan. It allows you to extract your thoughts onto paper so that you can begin to clear your mind and work out your direction and present your plan.

- **Investor's Investment Protocol.** The investment protocol is a standard formatted procedure and style used for the investment deck and/or presentation of the investment to your investors. It establishes a standard format, a protocol that they become familiar with. It helps build rapport and trust, which are essential because we have found that once you get an investor to provide money and if you're successful in generating the projected return, there is a very high chance that the investor will be back for the next one. And this is the name of the game—happy investor, happy life. Form a group of 100 investors, and they are your "go to" for funds. These are the investors that will give you free advertising like when you go to a good movie or a restaurant and you can't wait to tell your friends about it.

- **Investment Presentation Deck.** To put the magic touch on your presentation and investment plan, at minimum put together a basic PowerPoint presentation with some background information on you, your company, and the key attributes of the investment. This makes you look really good and makes it easier for you when raising money. And once you do one, you have a template to customize for each of your projects that need a little extra to throw your hat over the fence. Templates are available in the online Modern Wealth Building Formula curriculum.

Now, I want to be very clear that this is not faking it till you make it. It's a form of preparation meeting opportunity that gives you the same result as faking it till you make it. It involves Confidence, Competence, and an Optimistic Mindset. With these critical elements in place, there is not much you won't seek to understand moving forward. And once you complete your first investor's plan, protocol, and deck presentation to an investor, you have broken the ice and you are ready to ROCK 'N' ROLL with a template that you can customize for many million-dollar presentations. So let's get a better understanding of the capital components.

Understanding Equity

The two types of equity are Common Equity and Preferred Equity. Neither is the type of equity you gain in your home as you pay off the mortgage. In this context, equity is the money invested in an investment property for an ownership interest with a projected rate of return on the investment.

Common Equity. When you invest in a common equity position, you essentially gain ownership interest in the property in the form of a limited liability company with potential for growth. You stand to profit if the property value increases along with annual distributions.

There is most often preferred equity and a third-party debt lender on the property whose debt interests are the senior interests and paid back first where common equity is more of a seed capital. The most senior interest in the investment (usually the bank) always has priority in the return on their investment. There is no deal where a bank will allow you take profits until they're paid in full. In other words, the common equity investment is typically an early-on investment at a higher risk (and a higher rate of return or interest rate because of that risk) than a debt lender because the debt lender gets paid back first.

Preferred Equity. This is a general term for any investment. It is widely used to describe a specific type of equity investment in real estate. The preferred equity position is also typically converted into an ownership interest ("equity") in real estate that can be in various entity structures. These structures include and are not limited to Limited Partnerships and Limited Liability Companies.

In return for these equity interest positions, the investors are entitled to either a fixed rate of return and/or ownership interest and distribution based on the percentage of ownership in the investment.

For example, if your ownership interest is 20 percent, and the net profit is $100,000, your distribution will be $20,000.

On larger projects where syndication is prevalent, the entity that owns the investment property will usually have different types of equity investors and debt lenders. In these capital stacks, preferred equity ranks senior to common equity, but it ranks junior to the debt used to finance the real estate project. In other words, when the property generates income from rent or profits when the property is sold, preferred equity holders are paid after the debt lenders but before common equity holders.

Understanding Debt

Two types of debt are relevant to our capital conversation: Mezzanine Debt (or interim debt) and Senior Debt. Let's discuss each in greater detail.

Mezzanine Debt (Interim Debt). This type of debt bridges the gap during a risky part of the process, when you want to lock up a deal but aren't quite ready because you haven't completed your due diligence. This type of high-interest debt is used as a last resort so you don't lose a golden opportunity. But this can get dicey because you may have to extend the property hold period with a mezzanine loan and incur more costs.

Now, if you compare between mezzanine debt and equity financing, it's one of the highest-risk forms of debt. The primary difference between primary equity and mezzanine debt is generally that mezzanine debt is a loan that can be secured by a lien on the property while preferred equity is an equity investment in the property with ownership in the investment entity.

In relation to the payment priority, these loans are subordinate to senior debt but senior to preferred equity. This means that they offer some of the highest returns when compared to other debt types. Both mezzanine debt and preferred equity can be an effective form of capital that allows higher leverage (senior debt loan to value) to the borrower at a lower cost than common equity. In return, the investors in the mezzanine position in the capital stack have a more secured position relative to the equity but a higher yield for their additional risk in being subordinate to the senior loan.

Senior Debt. This is the steak and potatoes for banks. However, an individual investor or company can also take on a senior debt position. In most capital stacks, the senior debt is, at minimum, 60-65 percent of the total investment cost. It usually makes the most sense to leverage a minimum amount of your own money if you are not in this business full time. In the current low-interest rate environment, many investors seek these opportunities to achieve higher yields in lieu of traditional investment options.

In the case of renovations or new development, it's attractive to maximize the amount of loan being low-rate debt when given in the form of a construction loan. When the renovation or new construction is complete, the construction or improvement loan is taken out by the permanent mortgage. You might ask, "How do banks earn in such a competitive money market?" The main reason for this: Banks have incredibly low funding costs. They rely heavily on their bread and butter retail deposits, which are your checking and savings account essentially paying a minuscule interest rate. And we can follow the business model of lending this money out at a low rate, say at 3 to 8 percent, where lenders earn a profit on the spread between interest rates on retail deposits when senior in construction and permanent take-out loans. From my perspective, this is a hefty profit for not lifting a hammer.

The Relationship between Debt and Equity

The relationship of equity to debt in real estate is a measure of Ownership where if the ratio is 60/40, the bank owns 60 percent of the value of your property. This ratio is also used to determine the amount of equity versus debt by the Loan to Value Ratio (LTV). For example, if the LTV is 75 percent on a $100,000 purchase price, the loan amount is maximized to 75 percent of the purchase price, which is $75,000, the loan amount over the value to give you the ratio. Then you can easily determine the balance to close on the property, 25 percent of $100,000, which is equity in the amount of $25,000. The equity and debt are the two parts of the capital stack and contingent upon the parameters of the deal.

Risk Levels in the Capital Stack

In determining the risk levels for capital stacking on equity and debt, note that common equity is your riskiest interest for yourself or an investor in the stack but that it earns the highest returns to compensate for the highest risk that can range between 10 to 20 percent. Preferred equity is less risky because of the hierarchy for both the raise and return. It provides rates of return that range from 6 to 12 percent. Lastly, we have the debt vehicles, where mezzanine debt has similarity with preferred return in the context of returns. However, senior debt is the least risky and most of the time is obtained when the shovel is ready to go into the ground or as the last component of the stack in any major investment as shown in the illustration that follows.

CAPITAL STACK

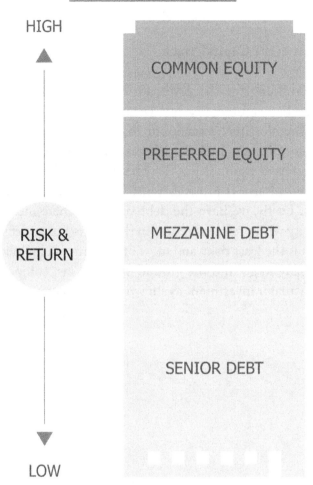

Debt Lending Vehicles

In a capital stack, the components can have multiple equity and senior debt positions that include several debt lending vehicles for consideration:

Transactional Funding. This is a specialized type of funding for real estate, ideal for quick house flips or wholesale deals where investors turn around properties without doing anything. Transactional funding immediately solves this issue by allowing investors to purchase properties with no money provided there is an assignment of the contract, an end buyer in place to purchase the property within a short time frame, usually two to five days.

Private Lending. This is when individuals lend their own money to other investors or managed real estate funds while securing a loan or note with a mortgage on the property or an interest in the investment. Essentially, private funding is a viable alternative to traditional lending institutions, like big banks.

Hard Money. This is a specific type of asset-based lending through which a borrower receives funds on real property. Private investors or companies typically issue short-term hard money loans. Interest rates are typically much higher than conventional loans because of the higher risk and shorter investment duration.

Fix and Flip Rehab Funding. This has a variety of resources to fill the pot of gold at the end of the rainbow. These include family and friends, finance partners, home equity loans, 401(k) loans, personal loans, and seller finance or business lines of credit.

Mezzanine Loans. Previously described, this can be a hybrid of debt and equity that gives the lender the rights to convert to an equity interest in the case of default, generally after senior debt is paid.

Institutional Lenders. This will provide finance for both commercial and residential real estate in scenarios that include purchases by individuals and companies for their own purpose and for income-producing real estate investments.

Show me the money! Now that we better understand the type of equity and debt available to investors, as well as the manner in which we can FUND projects, let's focus on how to FACILITATE what you are about ready to fund.

The Third Step: FACILITATE

You might ask, "What does facilitation have to do with real estate?" Good question. In my terms, FACILITATE encompasses the full spectrum of a real estate investment transaction, the entire process from the initial phone call through stabilization (the line to cross for profit) on the investment. It triggers where you begin. It includes an analysis of the deal to verify the numbers and the know-how to make an offer with ideal terms. With these technicalities in mind, you also want to facilitate with enthusiasm in spearheading the due diligence process, take actions to minimize risk, and have the capacity to close deals. And to ice the cake, you want to analyze and present continuous flow of feasible deals to pack the pipeline for the investors. That is what great facilitators often do. In brief, it's your ability to facilitate the process no matter the acquisition type and the operations necessary to execute and exit strategies required to fulfill your investment criteria.

A day in the life of any real estate investor requires absorbing knowledge like a sponge with continuous and never-ending improvement on a personal level. It's a mountain you are climbing, which requires constant openmindedness to change, flexibility to accept recommendations, and continuous implementation of new systems to become more effective. It forces you to attain the ability to course correct like a chameleon. Remember, as you increase the play of your game, you MUST expand your thinking, add tools to your tool belt, and implement systems for efficiency to continuously measure improvement in the overall effectiveness of your operation.

For example, imagine yourself in position for a big deal. You have boots on the ground with trained deal finders on the hunt, dream team players in place to support your mission, and investors fully on board! You guessed it, the phone rings. The caller ID says, "Jennifer Dawkins." It's the real estate broker you just met and are counting on. You're ready and have been waiting for this moment your entire life. You grab a pad and answer the phone.

"Hello. How are you? What's happening?"

"Did you receive my message about that property in _____?"

"No, tell me more."

"It's a hot off-market deal that may meet your criteria mentioned. Can you take a look at it?"

It's that simple.

Let's view this thought process as if you're in the business. The phone conversation may help you gather information for your investment feasibility evaluation to see if the investment will work for you. In many cases, the information needed to fully evaluate the investment is sparse on off-market deals and requires some digging. For example, the required data in a residential two- to four-family investment property would typically include location, rent roll, and price depending on the resources and whether it's listed on the market or as an off-market deal. In some cases, the deal is so hot that your deal hunter is still gathering reconnaissance and requires you to jump on board—all hands-on deck—to help with gathering data to analyze and make the deal happen. This is right where you want to be, with unlimited possibilities and your plan moving into execution. So what's next?

Now that you know that information alone does not suffice, what's required for you to take action toward locking up the deal? Let's assume this is not the case of sparse information because you received a call from your trained agent who has learned your criteria and knows exactly what you are looking for. In this case, there is no need to raise your guard until you get to know them. You simply move forward without analysis. However, in all cases, you must do property research to either find or confirm data around the investment information we are going to discuss further.

In this case, where a trained team member calls, it often saves you time and money on research and collecting data because they already know what you are looking for and they understand your investment criteria. In many cases, they bring you the data you need to evaluate the deal. So, as far as you're concerned, this is a profitable deal that you need to clarify and verify. It's now a matter of confirmation of the investment parameters and that they meet your criteria so that you can pull the trigger.

Regardless, with any real estate deal, as we mentioned in the investment criteria section, you execute actions to inspect the following property attributes with all team members to flush out any issues related to due diligence:

1. Location
2. Price
3. Property Size
4. Unit Configuration
5. Building Square Footing
6. MEP (Mechanical, Electrical, and Plumbing) Systems
7. Existing Debt
8. Status of Seller
9. Occupants
10. Neighborhood
11. Flood Zone
12. Oil Tank
13. Owner Finance
14. Estimated Repair Costs
15. ARV – After Repair Value
16. Title Search
17. Environmental Impact
18. Building Requirements
19. Zoning Ordinance
20. Comparables

The value you obtain in looking closely at these items is directly related to loss prevention. This is the process and the repetitive points of review in developing an internal checklist that acts as an insurance policy to ensure you don't miss anything when you're following our vetting protocol.

Now that you have the crucial data in front of you, you can implement a five-step process to determine the potential success of any deal or whether or not you should FACILITATE it. This truly is facilitation in motion, and it will lead you to the path of closing the deal. Here are the five main steps my clients use and that I apply in the heat of the moment.

The steps to FACILITATION mastery are as follows:

1. Paper Napkin Analysis. Is dinner being served? "What the heck is this?" you might ask. It's a phrase I coined after learning how to analyze a real estate deal in my studies at New York University and then computing the numbers for my first deal on the back of a paper napkin. I will always remember my professor telling us that you must do the calculations longhand before you start plugging numbers into a spreadsheet or you will make a mistake. That was 1998, well before abandoning your old green accounting sheets was an option. So, in other words, I like to run some simple numbers on a piece of paper, longhand, to determine what next step to consider before I start plugging data into a financial model. The paper napkin analysis works perfectly if you want to quickly determine if a potential deal meets the threshold of your investment criteria. Once I determine that the rough numbers meet my criteria, I then begin to dress up the act. The data is then put into a financial model that spits out the investment criteria detail in a much more presentable format for you to talk turkey.

And to the extent of the level of financial feasibility analysis, it will depend on the size of the project and type of project. On a deal with a buy-and-sell exit strategy, the financial feasibility analysis may be much less sophisticated with a down-and-dirty profit and cash-and-cash return on investment. Contrast that with a buy-and-hold approach, where you have cash-on-cash projections at stabilization, a ten-year cash flow spreadsheet, and an internal rate of return, and it may require a few more skill sets to meet your presentation goal. Nothing to sweat—there are dozens of programs and people that can help you with your more sophisticated financial modeling.

2. Due Diligence. This is a key to investment success but can be time consuming. In fact, it can be time restrictive on many occasions. Therefore, you must be creative if you are being squeezed into a corner by the seller without enough time to conduct a thorough due diligence. When this occurs, certain terms and conditions must be put in the contract that will allow you to extend the period for a price to ensure you maintain your fiduciary responsibility to your investors by not losing the deal. What do I mean? I mean that you need to negotiate a term that allows a period of time to perform due diligence to be conducted without losing your deposit or agreeing to allow a portion of your deposit to go hard (nonrefundable) to extend the hold period for another six months.

The most important aspect in this process is to ensure that you're not emotionally attached to the investment, trying to make it work by fitting a square in a round hole, but instead taking great caution to second-guess yourself and the property data that has been obtained from any source relative to the transaction. The process typically includes the performance of financial feasibility calculations, evaluation of market conditions and comparable values (location, location, location), review of property documents, including tax history, flood zone, legal, and building department documents, to name a few.

- Physical inspection at property and structure. This is where you or someone on your team walks the land and enters the property. In the case of our example just mentioned, you want to review the property due diligence checklist and look for any signs of oil tanks, which is the most risk based on potential soil and water contamination. If you are remote, you must have your field reconnaissance person take pictures of electrical panels and meters, HVAC equipment, house elevations, the streetscape, and the kitchen and baths and post findings into a database for information retrieval by analysts for pricing and property evaluation.
- Financial analysis of the numbers. You need to know what your projected profits are, of course, and your slice of the pie. Since we talked all about finding profitable deals, your system must immediately filter deals that are not at minimum 70 percent of the market value.
- Insurance requirements. Verify that property is not in a flood zone or in any high hazard area, i.e. hurricanes, fires, mudslides, etc. And verify that insurance is available on any property you buy before you close on the property.
- Title, deed, and encumbrances. You want to know of any encumbrances preventing you from taking control especially

when tenants are living in the property and most importantly in the case of buying foreclosures.

- Building department. If you see there have been improvements made on the property, visit the local building department to verify that proper permits were filed for and executed upon. We've been in situations where we have purchased homes with improvements unbeknownst to the building inspector, and when it was time to start project inspections, the inspector called us on it, which equated to an avoidable expense.
- Foreclosure attorney. Call the foreclosing attorney on all foreclosure deals. You never know what you will find out, and it can save your shirt. I can't tell you how important this is when buying foreclosures. Talk through the public notice and make sure there are no hidden liens, utility payments, and/or condo fees, etc.
- Homeowners' Fees. If a condominium association is part of transactions, make sure you find out the amount in arrears. This can be costly, and it's not public information. You should assume there is a problem with condo fees 100 percent of the time because if they are not paying their mortgage, they are not paying condominium fees.

In our real estate development process, we have a long laundry list of due diligence items— anywhere from thirty to fifty—for various types of projects that we verify before making an offer. The due diligence and inspections are critical steps to prevent pitfalls and mistakes that could be avoided and reduce profits.

3. Locking Up the Deal. Assuming that the deal is right for you, this may be a no-brainer. On the other hand, you might be chomping at the bit. Either way it's the critical step to get into the game, and you might want to go hang out with some deal junkies to get rid of any fear. You know the type of dealmaker I'm talking about—they will throw in their mother and her cooking to lock up the deal. All kidding aside, you must get control of the property to apply the methods you have learned and have been waiting to deploy. This is the part of the process that I've chosen to stick my neck in when acquiring property even though my team is on the case. It requires all focus and gives you another set of eyes.

From the outset, you must begin to think like this and familiarize yourself with some basic terms of a letter of intent because in many cases, you often wait on a whole slew of things from various people to lock up a deal. It's a bit of a fast-tracking game, and someone must spearhead the effort while others vet and inspect the property. However, in any case, you and/or your buyers should be trained to be a walking Letter of Intent (LOI).

Therefore, I'm fully prepared to generate an LOI with business terms where the attorneys are out of it until we figure out the business terms and control the property. I'm not saying I don't continuously consult with an attorney through this process. It's just that in some cases when dealing with a seller who does not want counsel involved, you must do what it takes to get a deal done. Even on larger deals, a letter of intent and proof of funds have been written to seal the deal.

4. Investor Presentation. I'll say it again—presentation, presentation, presentation. It's everything, so take the time necessary to nail it. Establishing a consistent presentation for your investors has worked for me so consider my suggestion on protocol. This is where all your hard work comes into play and the stage where it becomes just another deal. There is no need to be nervous because you have positioned yourself with investors whom you've prepared with the understanding of a mutual investment criteria, long-term real estate market strategy, and common opportunistic goals. They are waiting for the next deal, and it's now a simple standard operating procedure for your next presentation.

Most investors are savvy and don't have a lot of time to dwell. They know what they want—less is better. Therefore, the investment presentation package, in my opinion, should be executive style, direct, and to the point. You have one objective—present the investment (your challenge) along with the solution that mutually benefits both parties, with a brief description of the raise, facilitation through stabilization, and the exit strategy, i.e. sell, hold, syndicate, refinance, etc.

Tell them the plan, show the numbers behind it, and then tell the long-term exit strategy. Keep it simple in most cases, and always be prepared to take your presentation to the next level if you see bigger deals on the horizon. It's also important to use listening skills without your filter. Listen openly to investor feedback (not the voice in your head) so that you can improve the presentation as required based on specific investor feedback and any market factors. Now it becomes routine. The investors have seen repetition and consistency in results, they are familiar with the numbers, and they are comfortable that the investment meets the investment criteria. If they request additional information, you can present your due diligence, steps to closing, and operating agreement all in preparation to collect your funds.

5. Invest and Close Transaction. It's showtime! You got this, and it's always a proud feeling on closing day. That's right, I did it! It's not always about the money on some closing days. I'm sure most of you have been down to ramen noodles or cereal, praying for no last-minute hiccups on closing day. The stomach butterflies are unbearable at times. As you do this more often, the nervousness becomes less and it becomes a standard operating procedure. Just another day in paradise!

No, seriously, we view the real estate investment world as a bit of a game, especially me, being a former all-state high school and college football player. In this context, where are you in the game? How do you view a closing when complete? Do you look back and talk with the team about what was done well and worked? What didn't work? What we could have done better? This applies back to the measuring performance we discussed and the continuous and never-ending improvement that we suggest as a habit you gain. What just came to mind from my son's impeccable discipline as a US Marine intelligence officer is your own periodic AAR, an *after action report* to measure your performance and improve upon the results.

Also ask yourself this: Are you always on the field, or are you in the stands watching the game? Consider at times we switch back and forth and we wonder why our goals didn't evolve. Many moving parts and people in the process are drifting in life or analogized as sitting in the stands watching the game they want to play; therefore, it's your duty to stay on the field and engage fully in the game, even when you are at the highest level while your team is responsible for the details of the transaction.

So let's get to the point of this section. You obviously placed an earnest deposit to control the property. You spent money and time in due diligence, and now it's time to prepare for the closing. The transaction may be a quick-turn assignment of the contract, it could be a fix and flip, improve and hold, entitlement play on new development, an abandoned building planned for conversion, or a multiunit. In all cases, preparation for the closing relies now on counsel and appropriate dream team players to be the final sets of eyes on both the business (second-guess my assumptions) and to consider any implications from various perspectives. I choose to not be penny wise and dollar foolish in learning my lesson. There is nothing like a punch in the gut at the closing to realize your team dropped the ball and you are making less money than anticipated or learning that money has already been spent. It happens, and that's why I emphasize precision in anything you do. Don't cut corners. My methodology pays off in the long run. The way you would do anything for yourself is the way you do everything.

Time is money, and if you don't consider my advice on precision in establishing how it gets done you may find that tasks take additional iterations when not necessary, which is a loss in efficiency and the overall effectiveness of the process. For instance, do you want to do things thrice or find the cake half-baked? The cake does not taste good when the inside is still paste. It does make sense, and we have learned not to take this shortcut or be attracted to the shortcut time-savings illusion. I know this from being a semiprofessional magician—there are many illusions in life. Don't let the eye trick you.

The five steps just outlined to help you achieve Facilitation Mastery are essential to assisting you with completing a transaction and managing a real estate portfolio. Without familiarity with these steps and working with a mentor or surrounding yourself with a dream team that watches your back, you will not reduce risk and become aware of the small margin for error in real estate and your exposure to risk. This is not a business you want to crack your teeth on by trying this by yourself; and you want to understand the differences between commercial and residential real estate investing so that you can formulate a strategy, to be discussed in our next chapter.

The devil is truly in the details, but the opportunities are literally everywhere. Applying the Modern Wealth Building Formula can absolutely position you and your investment portfolio in a place to succeed. We start by shifting our mindset and actually believing in our respective abilities to generate great opportunities to build wealth. Then we can utilize each of the three steps...

1. FIND
2. FUND
3. FACILITATE

to find the right deal, fund it and then facilitate it to closing. Once we do that, we are opening a treasure chest of possibilities. Exploring those opportunities is the topic of the next chapter.

When money realizes that it is in good hands, it wants to stay and multiply in those hands.

Idowu Koyenikan, *consultant and author*

CHAPTER 4

COMMERCIAL VERSUS RESIDENTIAL REAL ESTATE:
Making the Right Choice for Your Portfolio

Now that we have outlined the crucial steps to take to FIND, FUND, and FACILITATE different types of real estate transactions, let's apply these helpful theories to the two predominant types of real estate investing, Commercial and Residential Real Estate. Each of these has its own set of pros and cons, and it is important to determine which will be the best fit for your money and your portfolio. To do so, let's start by defining each in greater detail.

Commercial vs. Residential Real Estate

The main difference between commercial and residential real estate is the use, management style, and cost. Commercial properties are primarily used for a large range of business types. These investment properties can vary in use, such as medical facilities, office buildings, strip malls, shopping centers, and/or storefronts, just to name a few. Typical commercial property owners invest their money with the expectation to secure a certain return on their investment.

On the other hand, residential properties are typically used to house occupants. Normally, they serve as the owner's personal residence or as a property where a person pays rent to the owner. Similar to owners of commercial properties, residential owners typically buy homes to secure a return or to live in the property to raise their family. In most cases, these types of investors eventually see the value of their home increase. They then figure, why not buy another one? That's typically how it begins. One becomes two, and so on and so forth.

Both commercial and residential real estate can be a valuable part of your portfolio. Choosing the right one for you should often be based on your lifestyle, financial situation, and retirement goals. Many people have a second home, a two- or four-family dwelling that brings extra income into the primary residence. Either way, there is great opportunity in these investments. Let's look at each one in greater depth.

Commercial Real Estate

Commercial real estate includes office buildings, medical centers, hotels, malls, retail stores, farmland, multifamily housing, warehouses, and garages. Investors purchase these properties to produce income, typically from a tenant that leases the property for his or her business. Commercial real estate includes just about anything that has the potential to create passive income, from land to residential skyscrapers with a retail component on the first floor, the three-story suburban office building with covered parking, a local strip mall that has the bagel and stationery store, main street storefronts with the old-fashioned drug store, and the two-family duplex for city folks.

From the business perspective of the tenants that lease these properties, you could be buying and/or investing in several types of properties that house businesses in finance, manufacturing, government, medicine, and hospitality, to name a few. Corporations need space for corporate offices, industrial warehouses are necessary to store manufactured products, multifamily units are needed for residential living, and professionals need office space. To break this down in greater detail, I've categorized commercial investments as follows: land, multifamily, office properties, retail, industrial, and "special projects," a catch-all category that includes everything else:

- **Land.** Vacant land zoned for future redevelopment is ideal and just waiting for you to build a structure on it. Greenland, brownfields, vacant suburban land, you name it. They are what I call "land banks" waiting for you to dial in the combination to the safe.
- **Multifamily (Five Units or More).** This consists of small multifamily units, midrise apartment complexes, and high-rise condominiums. Small multifamily investments can include anywhere from five to ten units. Midrise apartment complexes are between five to nine stories. Apartment complexes are often between three to four structures. High-rises are ten stories and above with typically 100 units. They can also include three to four-story garden apartments without elevators that you also see more in urban areas along with smaller multifamily dwellings.
- **Office Properties.** These are classified as class A, B, and C space, with A being the best quality space. C class is often older, poorly located, and often in need of extensive renovation and infrastructure updates. Commercial office properties can include single-tenant buildings, small professional buildings, skyscrapers, and everything in between.
- **Retail.** This can be freestanding, like a bank or a restaurant. It is often found on lower floors of residential towers and office buildings. The more familiar retail types may be strip centers, community centers, power centers, and regional malls.
  - **Strip Centers.** These are spread on neighbor retail sites from 5,000 to 100,000 square feet that have an anchor tenant to draw customers, mixed with smaller retail units, perhaps a restaurant, pet store, hair salon, or a specialty store.
  - **Community Centers.** These contain larger sites for centers between 150,000 and 350,000 square feet of commercial space and include multiple anchors like Target, Marshalls, or Sears. Also, they can include grocery stores like Whole Foods, drugstores, office supply stores like OfficeMax, and fitness centers like

LA Boxing, etc.

- **Power Centers.** These contain big-box retailers as anchor tenants like one in my neighborhood that has a Walmart and Home Depot, with each anchor occupying between 30,000 and 200,000 square feet within the power center. There are also freestanding retail units that include a variety of restaurants and shopping stores.
- **Regional Malls.** They vary in size from 400,000 to two million square feet. They have several anchor tenants like Lord & Taylor, Neiman Marcus, Macy's, Apple, restaurants and food courts, and many large, medium, and small stores.

- **Industrial.** From warehouses to large manufacturing sites, industrial buildings are typically used for manufacturing industries, and now data storage, as they offer spaces inexpensively compared to offices with higher height specifications and docking availability. These types of properties often lend themselves more to investment properties to fill the demand.
- **Special Projects.** This catch-all category would include any other nonresidential, retail, and commercial property just listed, such as hotel, resort, hospitality, and medical and self-storage facilities as well as golf ranges, sports facilities, car washes, etc.[2]

Residential Real Estate

Residential real estate is essentially real estate purchased as a primary residence. There is much controversy as to whether you can even consider this type of acquisition an investment property when you reside in the home. Home ownership is like a freight train. You have to decide whether you want to jump onto the speeding train with a great chance to get the ride of your life, or you can continue to watch the train scream on by. The variety of residential real estate uses, primarily for your personal residence or investment use, include:

- **Single-family Houses.** This is usually a standalone house built on a single lot without the owner having to share the land with anyone else, as opposed to a multifamily house. This could vary slightly in city buildings, where the unit owner shares a wall, known as a party wall, but the unit still has all other exclusive uses, such as direct entry off street level and separate utilities.
- **Multifamily Houses.** These usually range in size from two to four units, with separate living units. They may include duplexes (attached side-by-side with separate entrances) or a fourplex, essentially the same as two- to four-family units. These layouts are more normal in cities where lot widths are as small as twenty-five feet wide. And anything larger than four units is considered commercial property from a loan finance perspective.
- **Condominiums.** These are single, privately owned units within larger multiunit buildings or communities. They are similar to the structure of midrises, high-rises, and apartment buildings. Together with other unit owners, owners own the land and common areas like the lobby, stairs, hallways, mechanical space, elevators, roof, etc. In addition, they share the maintenance expenses, typically in the form of a monthly maintenance and condominium fee.
- **Townhomes.** These are units that are usually larger in square footage than condos and are side-by-side, like a duplex or fourplex, and are two stories or taller with a garage and small front yard. Even though residents still share walls with one or two other buildings, they own their interior space, exterior walls, and roof. Similar to a single-family home, residents have their own utilities and homeowner's insurance policy for their home and property.
- **Cooperatives.** These are units within one multiunit building where everyone living in the building owns shares in it, and a contract or lease with a corporation allows the owner to occupy the unit. This cooperative structure is typical in major cities and some of the biggest addresses in the world. Nowadays, there is a major shift in the value and sales of co-ops based on competition

from the vast number of condominium developments with new technology and flashy amenities, especially in New York City.

• **Vacation or Short-Term Rentals.** These are also a type of buy-and-hold property, but they are used for your vacation home or short-term rentals. We have many of these types of properties in New Jersey, which you may have seen on the show *Jersey Shore*.

Fundamental Differences

Besides actual use, a few other differences exist between residential and commercial properties. The transactions are different because different rules govern them. From purchase to closing, residential transactions are well established. The time it takes to purchase a home is often dictated by the buyer's mortgage approval and their ability to obtain financing in a timely period.

Typically, the buyer makes an offer, and then a counteroffer may occur, after which a contract is signed with an earnest deposit. The mortgage underwriting approval and due diligence process now begins, which may include home, termite, and radon inspections and the appraisal, property survey, and title policy prepared for the closing. This process normally takes thirty to sixty days.

Commercial mortgages typically are much more stringent, have much higher requirements in terms of credit scores, require a larger cash down payment, and have higher interest rates and shorter payback periods. In addition, you must have prior experience and be able to provide proof of funds and verify cash reserves.

Commercial properties include several parameters not included in residential real estate deals. The most prevalent is construction requirements where municipalities are governed by zoning areas that prevent the building of certain types of properties in certain areas in town. These are specified zoning areas designated by the city for specific building types based on access feasibility, traffic analysis, and environmental impact. This designation establishes zoning ordinances that control developers from running wild in an attempt to develop commercial properties in residential areas.

Construction codes for commercial properties typically include a much stricter set of rules, codes, and permits primarily due to the need for noncombustible construction. This is largely due to the level of structure complexity, safety codes, and the number of people who will be expected to utilize the space. There are also elevators and fire suppression and emergency requirements not included in residential construction, which require special inspections.

The due diligence process is also much longer for commercial deals. In some instances, this can take over one year. There is engineering, permitting, and many other due diligence items within a commercial real estate feasibility study that are contingencies for closing. This period of time and cost must be included in the financial analysis as one of the carry cost items anticipated at the outset.

With this new perspective and understanding of residential and commercial real estate, now let's look at the pros and cons of each.

The Pros and Cons

One question you might ask is, "What are the positive and negative aspects of real estate investing?" Or, you might say, "What investment strategy works best for me?" Let's look at a further comparison of commercial versus residential real estate and their respective investment purposes to understand more about the benefits for one type of investment versus the other. In doing so, you can make a more informed decision and pick the right investment strategy for you. From my experience, this upcoming perspective will guide you on the right strategy path or onto a stepping stone for the quantum leap in your existing real estate business for sure.

With the key of being certain with your uncertainty, understanding the pros and cons of each investment strategy will help you understand the risk. What do I mean? There is risk in real estate investing, which requires knowing the pros and cons that will inspire you to execute strategies with a calculated risk, and that's what you want. Therefore, here are general pros and cons for real estate in general.

Real Estate 101

In general, real estate is an extremely viable means to achieve financial freedom. That is why you are reading this book. Note that the pros and cons to follow equate to the benefits of getting into real estate. In addition, just based on the odds alone, with 90 percent of millionaires becoming millionaires through real estate, it makes sense to jump in and try your hand. If you plan on attending the game, you have to get out of the stands and walk onto the field. It's game time, and game on!

The Pros

- **Passive Income.** Monthly cash flow is the name of the game before pulling out of the driveway.
- **Control.** If you set up your plan properly and execute accordingly, you can control your destiny in real estate, have a minimal barrier to entry, don't need a formal education, and can control the properties.
- **Tax Benefits.** These are various deductions off your taxable income available to everyone and very beneficial for professionals trading time and making money. With these write-offs, your money works much better for you with real estate as an outstanding investment option.
- **Insured.** Similar to SEC protection on a stock investment, insurance helps you sleep at night knowing that your hard-earned savings is safe, as the property has insurance and is a reliable asset.

The Cons

- **Market Instability.** Markets are cyclical and have no guarantees. Therefore, I recommend area and market diversification.
- **Being a Landlord.** Most people don't have the first idea about managing property, and therefore they shy away from real estate investing. Keep in mind, for a small fee you can find a

property manager to manage your asset, so let's not sweat the small stuff.

- **Raising Money.** This can be stressful and remind you of a live presentation in public speaking. This is one of the biggest fears for people surveyed about one of the toughest things to do. The reward outweighs the fear, and it just takes the first step.
- **Vacancy.** Cash flow issues can arise when you have vacancies, and therefore this a good reason to have multiunit properties in lieu of single-family properties in the event that the tenants move out. In the latter, you are left with nothing coming in, whereas with multiunits, the hit is less impactful with other tenants in place.
- **Due Diligence.** This can be a pain in the ass if you don't have the stamina. It requires patience and tenacity to get it done, or you simply have to find someone who's good at it. There is always a way.

With this general understanding of real estate pros and cons, you are now ready to look deeper into the pros and cons of commercial versus residential investing.

Commercial Real Estate

Commercial real estate investing is the major leagues of real estate, as you could invest as little as $100,000 and well north of $100 million. Therefore, I don't have to say that the margin for error is much smaller, the potential losses are much higher, and you better know what you're doing at this level. Or you will lose everything.

Let's look at more specific pros and cons of commercial and residential real estate investing:

The Pros

- **Higher Returns.** One of the advantages of investing in commercial real estate is greater returns. Single-family investments typically offer an annual return of between 1 to 6 percent, while commercial real estate offers returns between 6 to12 percent.

- **Longer Lease Terms.** Due to long-term business goals of the owner to establish stabilization along with sustainability, commercial leases could be five to ten to ninety-nine-year land leases opposite of terms for residential leases, which are typically one year.
- **Hours of Operation.** In many cases, your tenants will operate during the normal working hours of nine to five, therefore you can expect fewer calls in the middle of the night if you own several multiunit investments versus commercial investments.
- **Aligned Interests.** An important factor in the bigger scheme of things is that owners have the same aligned interest as commercial tenants. They keep up the property so that their business quarters are attractive, whereas in residential, you may be aware of how an apartment fares after a reckless tenant moves out.
- **1031 Exchange.** This applies to both commercial and residential where you can sell a rental property and invest in another "like kind" property without paying a capital gains tax.

The Cons

- **More Competition.** With all the buzz, the commercial market continues to thrive. Therefore, you may find it difficult to find a commercial property where the numbers pencil out, especially at the height of the market. If and when you do catch a fish on the hook, chances are high that there will be an increased competition to make a bid.
- **Larger Initial Investment.** Most commercial real estate investments are going to require much larger upfront capital due to the simple fact that you add a few zeros. This makes it more difficult to enter the market if you don't have the mindset to syndicate. Along with the additional initial capital, you are

likely to have soft costs in the case of a carry period or a real estate development.

- **Quality Professional Help.** This is a double-edged sword where you really don't have a choice to manage the property yourself unless you are in the property management business. At this level, you typically contract a major-league property manager to assist you in maintaining your commercial real estate property. Do not fail to perform extensive research on management companies in consideration, which will reinforce the notion that "you get what you pay for."

- **Zoning.** You can't just convert and pop up a commercial building in any neighborhood. Towns and cities have zoning ordinances that dictate where you can place a commercial investment, the characteristics thereof, and what your property is subject to.

- **Values Drop Sharply.** Changes in infrastructure or master planning can force values to drop sharply. We have positioned ourselves for major investments in areas only to immediately scale back when infrastructure or transportation deals fall through. This eliminated many future jobs, upset the master plan, and the property values were drastically affected.

- **Greater Risk.** One of the greatest risks associated with commercial real estate is when an investor does not understand the margin for error. When you're investing in commercial real estate of any magnitude, you want to become conscious of the pitfalls. In addition to the higher risk and margin for error, there is risk due to the visitors on the property grounds and within the building itself. In many cases, you may want to obtain specific types of additional insurance, i.e. key man, professional liability, etc.

- **Commercial Properties Are Sensitive to Economic Conditions.** When the economy is strong, businesses flourish and demand for commercial properties generally rises. But when there's an economic downturn, demand for commercial premises usually falls.

Residential Real Estate

Now let's unpack the pros and cons of investing in residential real estate.

The Pros

- **Easy Market Entry.** Residential is the least path of resistance to getting started in real estate, and from a financial perspective, it's much easier to obtain money and deposits are much smaller.
- **Higher Demands.** One of the most common investments and the easiest to purchase is the single-family home, which correlates to the $31.2 trillion housing value mentioned earlier.
- **Liquidity.** The biggest advantage of investing in a single-family home is liquidity. If an investor decides to diversify out of the single-family home business, the properties can easily be sold to homeowners or other investors.

The Cons

- **Higher Competition.** Since the pro is easy entry, there will be great competition in the residential market. Therefore, if you use the Modern Wealth Building Formula, you will differentiate yourself from the pack.
- **Minimal Income Streams.** The primary disadvantage to single-family homes as an investment strategy is that there is only one income stream from the tenant currently living in the home. If the tenant leaves, you have no other income to absorb the impact whereas with multifamily buildings, if one tenant leaves there are still at least one or more tenants paying rent.
- **Difficult Tenants.** Despite your thorough vetting of prospective renters, you can very easily wind up with tenants who are a disaster. For example, they could cause damage to the unit, not

pay rent, or be a constant pain in the ass, complaining about every little thing.

- **Lack of Liquidity.** Real estate is not an immediate liquid asset like stocks. Even in the hottest market, it can easily take several months to sell a property. If your timing is driven by the lack of cash flow or other unexpected events, your need to sell fast might force you to drop your pants on the price.

- **Rising Taxes and Insurance Premiums.** The interest and principal on your mortgage are typically fixed, but there is no guarantee that taxes and insurance will not increase at a higher rate than you can increase rents. Be aware of projected tax hikes and insurance premiums, as they can increase after natural disasters.

- **Neighborhood Decline.** If you are trying to keep up with the Joneses, that's great and not always the case with your neighbors. In an ideal scenario, neighbors have a mutual goal to maintain the value of their property. However, there are many cases where neighborhoods become distressed and property values go down. This causes neighborhoods to decline, and your investment could depreciate over time.

- **Landlord Duties.** Being a landlord is not for everyone. You may just be a shy person who finds it difficult to demand higher rents or face confrontation to protect your asset. In some cases, you have the opposite situation. For instance, my parents rented their home in New Jersey to tenants who eventually became friends and outstanding long-term tenants maintaining the property.

- **Maintenance.** Property maintenance is a preventive measure to prevent large outlays of cash because of neglect. Keep on top of maintaining your property, as it will help hold value and maintain stability to both the asset and neighborhood. Minor and major repairs will arise, and some property owners can save money and perform the work themselves. However, most investors, like myself, lack the time, tools, or skills for home repair.

- **Special Considerations.** Whether you are buying a primary home or a rental property, look at various long-term exit strategies in the event of unforeseen circumstances. One example is a variable interest rate mortgage, where the investor must consider refinancing at a certain stage of the investment to be competitive and to maintain cash flow and a rate of return to investors.

Make sure you apply the pros and cons when it comes to investing in pure residential real estate because there are really only two options: single-family and multifamily maxed out at four units if we stay within the mortgage classifications context.

Investors Style Matches Investment Type

By now, you must be asking yourself about your investment style or lifestyle that applies to an investment style or type. You are in the right place if you are considering stepping into the game, upping your game, or wondering how this all fits into a long-term real estate investment strategy.

Like most things in life, you have to try it to see how one strategy looks before you go change strategies or change your lifestyle. If you are serious about real estate investing after you feel out the day to day of the type of real estate investing you are interested in, you can start the process of elimination. At this stage, you might be asking these questions:

What type of investor is the best to invest in commercial real estate?

What type of investor is the best to invest in residential real estate?

The hands-on investor is possibly more geared toward a pure residential approach, easy entry, targeted at 100 doors. They have a plan, and they work until the mission is accomplished. If you're a professional trading time for money on the job, you might be a better fit for a hands-off passive approach and different levels of risk and control. Understanding the primary distinctions should leave you with a direction to either think further about or decide based on short- and long-term circumstances.

The Right Strategy for You

When it comes to your investment strategies toward residential and commercial, there are a few things to consider before you sway in one direction or the other. These include:

- **Cash.** You need to raise more cash to grow as you take on larger properties and add zeros to your bottom line, especially in multifamily and pure commercial real estate. This is a bit more calculated and can offer a higher reward.
- **Tenants.** Real estate investing is a people business. You will either be dealing with residents or commercial businesses as your tenants. This is part of the process you have to deal with; you have to learn how to either manage the process yourself or delegate responsibility so you can go on with your life and enjoy the passive income. If you are not a people person or not interested in communicating with people, then real estate may not be for you.
- **Leases.** While most residential leases are relatively cut-and-dried and dictated largely by templates of the industry, commercial leases offer much more complex terms and opportunity in your negotiations. Therefore, you need to understand that the residential leases are fairly easy to understand and implement and nothing of concern. The commercial lease, however, can be lengthy since it relates to many graduating cost factors and big-time bread and butter on your end. When setting up your nest egg for retirement, I recommend the help of a lawyer so you can take full advantage of your entitlements.

Before deciding on any real estate investment strategy, thoroughly understand what each strategy entails so that you have a full view of the focus and target. Take time to network, meet with industry leaders, and join real estate investment clubs to learn about investment strategies and to find potential partners with a similar mindset. Building a network of real estate professionals will help you prepare for any cycle.

Common Strategies across the Board

Now that you better understand the pros and cons, the highs and lows, you are positioned to begin applying the FIND, FUND, and FACILITATE mentality to investing. Here are some common strategies that will help you succeed in either arena.

FIND (Bird-dogging). This is another word for deal scout, or finding deals for others and for the deal junkie type that doesn't really like to do anything else other than be the connector. This is an excellent place to begin a career in real estate, especially if you're a real estate agent. Statistics show that the average real estate agent does not do well, and I believe that's because they don't have the forward outside of the box thinking as resourcefulness. Why would you not, from the outset, be equipped with knowledge, tools, and the ability to hunt down big and small deals?

Lock-up and Sell Contract (Wholesaling). Also, known as "quick turning," wholesaling is the business of finding good deals on investment properties and then reselling them quickly for a small markup. In our 136 deals in one year, we would sell the contract in an average of sixty-six days and make a cash-on-cash return on investment above 200 percent. The key is having a buyer's list and money in position to make quick acquisitions. If you're good at sales, you'll like wholesaling. But if the idea of sales makes you cringe, I'd look for different strategies.

Buy, Improve, and Sell (Fix and Flip). The fix-and-flip strategy is the business of finding properties that need work, doing the repairs, and reselling them at top dollar for a profit. Fix-and-flips are for investors looking for active, short-term investments to quickly make money. They are typically for an active investor who has his boots on the ground; however, we bring in passive investors on fix-and-flip properties frequently that are bought, renovated, and then sold. They are not a get-rich quick scheme, but if done correctly, both investors and you can quickly profit from this strategy.

Buy and Hold (Short and Long Term). This should be your long-term strategy in either residential or commercial real estate because these are the types of exit strategies that signal a good investment; that's because of the steady passive income and the opportunity to gain appreciation while executing your wealth-building plan. If looking for active, stable investments, buy and holds are the way to go.

This strategy involves buying and holding rental properties for short and long periods—short means perhaps one to five years, and long means forever when it's a cash cow. Often the purpose of this strategy is passive income and appreciation through remodeling, raising the rent, and decreasing expenses. Therefore, buying an investment property as a buy and hold requires extensive research about the market, neighborhood, and property expenses to ensure positive cash flow. If you do not do your research, you may find yourself losing money instead of earning it every month.

The short-term buy-and-hold strategy works very well for multi-unit apartment turnaround projects. It also works well for rentals in nice neighborhoods and appreciating markets and for properties that have an added value component by improvement or future development or low existing rent, as a few examples.

From a long-term perspective, this is the strategy of owning real estate with the intention of keeping it for the long haul. Commercial real estate is ideal from this perspective. The benefits of this play are identical to how a turtle wins a race, a slow and steady strategy that includes increased rental income, expense tax benefits, and appreciation increasing long-term value.

These are your keepers—the properties in the best locations, those that attract the best tenants and tend to appreciate the most over time. Why? Because not all buy-and-hold properties are the same. They can range from single-family homes to skyscrapers. Depending on location and potential cash flow, an investor might choose to rent out a single-family home to an entire family or rent out individual rooms for boarding at a weekly rate.

So What's It Gonna Be? The Blended Approach

I've taken a blended approach and would recommend it based on the levels of a diversified portfolio you can create by a variety of market sectors and in different areas.

If I were to describe how a nice blended (balanced) approach would look, it would be to buy a house or invest in a residential property to get started or to buy a multifamily unit and occupy it in the beginning. Think about it, you get the best of both worlds: a pad you can call your own, and you're collecting rent to help pay for expenses. Who's better than you?

Shoot to establish stability, systems for sustainability, and a long-term strategy for retirement. The steps to obtain these items are outlined in the previous chapter, where you applied the principles of FIND, FUND, and FACILITATE to help you acquire your first or next level property.

Once you are positioned with stability, you can begin to benefit from the value of holding both commercial and residential real estate. What benefits am I talking about? The benefits of tax advantage, diversification, and long-term wealth. In real estate, there is no down-side to a blended approach because you are in the game of real estate where you are following all the basic principles of investing in the stock market to protect your assets and to operate within your risk tolerance. The beauty of the blended approach is that it simulates a diversification, and by spreading your investment over various areas you minimize impact from market upset in a specific area and it gives you another level of diversification.

I started investing in real estate with a single home, and then I moved onto a more blended strategy after years of pure residential and major high-rise residential development. It was quite an extreme, however this very unusual approach helped me discover the top-down mentality. In doing both of these, I always focused on cash flow and passive income because the combination of those two things equals financial freedom.

You all know what cash flow is—constant money in your pocket.

But passive income on investment property means income without getting your hands dirty. It can be in the form of a deal you control or where you give money to someone else to make the investment happen for you. One way to do this is by working with a private placement for midsize deals or a Real Estate Investment Trust (REIT), which is essentially where investors pool their money to buy large real estate investments, such as malls, skyscrapers, or many single-family homes. Each investor gets a share of the profits and does very little work. These passive investments generally have higher returns and less risk.

Another way to passively invest in real estate is to lend your money to an investor looking for a property to flip. Why wouldn't an investor just go to a bank? It's difficult to get a loan for a property that is vacant and needs work. This loan is called a first trust deed investment. The investors should pay the 20 percent down payment and closing costs. As a lender, you would receive interest payments on the loan and a final payment at the end of the term. Your money is secured by the property. This is just one strategy available to you as you work to build a more blended and balanced real estate investing strategy.

You've now read through a detailed analysis of the different types of real estate investing as well as the pros and cons of each. Keep in mind that most investors either try and change their initial strategy or they combine different strategies at different times. For example, you may begin with pure residential, then transition into multifamily, then commercial long-term buy and holds, and finally, you may develop real estate and a few fix and flips on the side like I do.

There is no right or wrong answer. Don't worry if you try one strategy and realize it doesn't work for you. Strategy is a bit of trial and error as well as an entrepreneurial venture. Sometimes you have to try an investment type before realizing it's not for you. I've shifted my strategies a dozen times to figure out the best blended approach and strategies that succeed. In the next chapter, we'll focus on understanding your market and being the smartest investor with a competitive advantage.

"*Wealth is a planned result that requires productive work and dedication. The Tanakh says, 'The plans of the diligent lead only to abundance; but all who rush in arrive only at want.'*"

H.W. Charles, *investor and author*

CHAPTER 5

EVALUATING THE MARKET:

100 Data Points to Be the Smartest Investor and Have a Competitive Advantage

If you were in the CIA, would intel matter to you? Of course it would. You would never expect the CIA or FBI to stand idle if there was a threat to person or property. The same is true in real estate. Clearly there is not as much at stake, but I want you to recognize the amazing potential in using intel when making a decision. In real estate, you would want to know everything possible that could be at risk or concern to reduce risk, maximize potential, and increase profitability. This is where intel, data, and technology set you apart in making decisions and give you a competitive edge.

Whether you are headed into the residential or commercial real estate market, it is crucial to be aware of the real estate market analysis, also known in the residential world as Comparative Market Analysis (CMA). The real estate market analysis selects similar properties that were either recently sold or listed in the same geographical area for comparison. By comparing these properties and adjusting for minor differences, an estimate of value is made for the subject property. The comparative market analysis is not the same as a real estate appraisal even though they both establish a value; the market analysis is more about the competition. The primary difference is that the real estate appraisal sets the parameters for a mortgage while a comparative market analysis gives the seller or buyer an understanding of current market values.

Whether you are buying or selling property, you will most likely hear the terms *real estate market analysis* and *real estate appraisal* at some point. In fact, you might have already heard them and are not sure how they apply. Whether you need an appraisal or market analysis depends on your goals, and in some cases, you will need both.

In this chapter, I'll outline the differences between the real estate market analysis and real estate appraisal, the importance of each, the similarities between the two, and when to use one rather than the other. My hope in doing so is that you gain an insightful understanding and valuable tools that you can apply to your evaluation of the real estate market.

Real Estate Market Analysis

Real estate market analysis is a process in which a property's value is determined based on the real estate market's value of similar properties (or real estate comps) in the same geographical area. These comps are generally recently sold properties or properties listed for sale.

Typically, real estate comps are within a one- to three-mile radius from your investment property. In addition, the real estate market analysis considers only properties sold within six months of your listing. I would suggest you compare no less than three properties to ensure you have an accurate picture of your listing market.

Below are other factors you will want to include in your market analysis:
- Economic Factors
- Socioeconomic Factors
- Demographic Developments
- Local Supply and Demand
- Market Rates
- Capital Market Access

• Constitution Legislation

Importance of Real Estate Market Analysis

Real estate market analysis is considered one of the most important steps for any real estate transaction because it helps you determine the estimated value of the investment and the income on the property you're willing to buy, sell, or rent. In residential properties, you will most likely find several comparable properties that are similar to, but do not exactly match, your listing. In commercial properties, there will often be minimal comparables for you to consider. It all depends on the market sector and the location to determine what comparables are available at the time of acquisition.

In the case of residential properties, you might have a similar property with small deviations that can impact price. For example, a two-family house with three bedrooms, two bath may be a comparable with another two family with one extra bathroom and a finished basement. When this occurs, and an exact comparison is unavailable, you can interpolate the data to determine value. In other words, you can play around with the numbers, what ifs, and differences to estimate the true value of your property with accuracy.

In addition, market analysis is crucial in determining the listing price of your real estate property. By comparing your investment property to similar properties in the market, you can, relatively with patience, put a price on your investment property.

As important as the value of an investment property is, it is not the only thing to take into consideration when conducting a real estate market analysis. Below are other important factors in valuing the market for your property.

• **Location.** Location is one of the biggest aspects in the world of real estate investments. Location impacts the value of every property. I'll say it again, "Location, location, location." For example, any investment that is close to public transportation, schools, business centers, main roads, and public facilities is for sure a very hot investment in your local market.

- **Main Characteristics of the Investment Property.** One day I found myself investigating the main characteristics of a building with clients who were considering renting while their penthouse was under construction. They were looking for a midtown rental for two years to settle into New York City before moving into their new place. They asked me to join them on their visit to observe building characteristics and amenities. The agent provided a tour presenting amenities and the unit to support the $60,000 per month asking price. These characteristics included square footage, quantity of bedrooms and bathrooms, amenities, concierge services, outside space, etc.
- **Compare the Data.** There are also two nonphysical characteristics you should take into consideration during a real estate market analysis:
    - *Vacancy Rate:* The comparative property analysis also allows you to estimate vacancy rates and how this may affect your rental income. This in turn helps your competitive strategy on pricing of the monthly rental based on supply and demand in the market.
    - *Price per square foot:* Also known as PSF, this can vary dramatically. For example, in New York City, a condo price can vary anywhere from $1,200 to $10,000 per square foot. In this type of market, it's critical and sets an example about why it's so important to know that the price varies depending upon the square foot. If two real estate properties are different in size, the bigger property's price per square foot will be less than the smaller property. You must know this level of detailed information to be a savvy investor.
- **Analyze Comparison Values.** Real estate comps are a very popular term in real estate investing, and it is critical that real estate investors look at recently sold properties to determine the market value of the investment property before they decide to sell or buy.

Before moving on, it's very important that I reiterate that your real estate market analysis is subjective and only an estimate of the true market value. It is only one factor, and the figures are not always accurate and should not stand alone for evaluating an investment property where an appraisal is also recommended. Also keep in mind that unforeseen factors could affect the value of the investment and its market value in the future.

Therefore, we emphasize once again the importance and specifics around measuring. To project rate of return results for your investors and to set a basis to measure against later, you must measure here at the outset against other properties. This allows you to compare a more concise appraisal with the outcome down the road to determine if the property was the right investment for you.

In short, the comparative market analysis will not only assist you in making the right investment decision but it will, in many cases, save you from making a wrong decision. I learned this on my first deal when I had no experience and had to prepare a market analysis on the assisted living market in Bridgewater, New Jersey. I had no clue about how to conduct one. I certainly didn't know the purpose, and I didn't see the ultimate value in this case until that ah-ha moment.

The findings of our market study revealed that my facility that had 113 beds could be absorbed into the market. However, we were one of five facilities slated for the market and it was a race to the finish line. Two of the five were complete, and my project was in a horse race for the next 100 beds to hit the market. Thankfully, our market analysis was deemed positive as the market had over 1,500 people between seventy-seven and eighty-three years old as candidates to fill our beds.

The Difference Between Real Estate Market Analysis and Real Estate Appraisals

What's the difference between a real estate market analysis and a real estate appraisal? In simple terms, a real estate market analysis lets you know how much similar properties are worth in the same geographic area of the property you are selling or buying.

In contrast, the real estate appraisal is the value of an individual property determined by a licensed appraiser. The appraisal includes the value a lender relies on to determine the maximum loan amount to buy the property based on the loan to value parameter.

To be precise, they both require certain information, including information such as lot size, building square footage, conditions, number of floors, bedrooms, and bathrooms and whether the property has amenities. Another difference between the two is that one uses surrounding properties recently sold to help determine value, while the other is comprehensive and includes a market analysis within the appraisal plus several additional parameters. The market analysis depends heavily on how much like properties nearby have sold for and how long the property lingered on the market before the sale. This process is called a real estate comparative, a slightly more detailed write-up versus a typical comparative market analysis seen in pure residential real estate.

Which One Is Necessary?

The market analysis is valuable to establish a price range and gauge the final asking price. However, it's not a requirement to move forward in any direction of a real estate transaction. An appraisal will be required, especially if you are asking for bank funds. Lenders across the nation require a licensed appraisal to cover their risk. With respect to you being on the buyers' side, if the appraisal comes in below the purchase price and the bank limits the amount of your loan and/or debt on the property, you always have the option of paying additional deposit monies to move forward with the purchase.

Sellers can also reduce the price to match the appraised value rather than lose the sale. Or I've personally adjusted upward with a work-letter-type credit to juggle numbers to help when a buyer wants to leverage the investment with less equity and more debt.

In a nutshell, to effectively market or buy a property, a real estate market analysis is a great tool for making sure a property is in the ballpark regarding its listing price, but it is not required. A real estate appraisal, however, is required if a mortgage company will loan the money for the purchase. A smart investor uses both.

Evaluating the Market

Coming from a top-down thinking model, let's focus on market analysis of commercial real estate investments since most comparable market analyses for residential properties are done by real estate agents for free. Therefore, I'll focus on the commercial market analysis parameters and residential market analysis components so you are on top of both games.

Investing in real estate requires a certain knowledge of your chosen local markets. Just like coaching a football team, property sellers, property buyers, and landlords all must look at the game as offense, defense, and special teams. The coach can't just focus on offense to be a winner. In real estate, you can't just sit and wait until you are on the field. You need to always pay attention to the investment properties you are targeting. Take it from my experience, it can be very helpful and it makes sense if you are establishing your territory. It will provide you with realistic data from hands-on experience about what to really expect when you're renting, making an offer on, or listing a property in that market.

Commercial Market Analysis

Commercial market analysis reminds me of one of my favorite TV programs as a kid, *My Favorite Martian*. On the show, antennas would come out of Uncle Martin's head. In that moment, he was about to get power and focus. The same is true when it comes to market analysis. You have to get focused and better understand the common risks associated with commercial real estate.

My mindset these days on commercial market analysis coincides with a national view. Therefore, let's look at your ultimate goals and how you can best analyze and understand any market in the nation. With the technology and the ability to identify opportunities nationwide before your competition does, my approach would be to learn how to:

- Anticipate how US real estate markets will likely behave over the next ten years
- Recognize the economic factors driving local real estate markets
- Understand theories concerning the causes and consequences of market cycles

Evaluating real estate markets is designed to help real estate professionals evaluate property investments in terms of better understanding the economic factors that drive them. Real estate investors rely on this information to effectively operate without going out of business. It's a skill in itself that you may see more people in the residential area utilize because of the market trends, competitiveness, and oversaturation. Therefore, in your specialized selected economic markets, your operations must include tracking of the most real estate rents, vacancy, and prices.

Relying on high-quality data sources will help ensure that your commercial real estate market analysis is reliably supported. No matter what market or what size market you're working within, the necessary research and experts are available to assist, using the same strategies from different sources. Whether you're an investor, broker, or builder like me, possessing a full understanding of the commercial real estate market can enhance your deal-making acumen, funding capacity, and facilitation mastery.

Your analysis of a particular property to buy or sell should include a definition of the market from a geographical perspective, learning more about values in that area, finding property sales volume, and analyzing any zoning, regulations, and even the master plans of a given town. Download market reports, and reach out to local experts.

A commercial real estate market analysis can allow you to gain a deeper understanding of your target asset class, location, and a bevy of market trends and forecasts. As noted, when I started developing a ninety-unit assisted living facility, I discovered the importance of the market analysis, which was conducted for a five- and ten-mile radius to determine the available market of people ages seventy-seven to eighty-three. We wanted to identify if the demographics were high enough to support 500 beds in the five-mile radius. It was an awakening to see that we could pinpoint the amount of people and our potential residents prior to even breaking ground.

Through all of this, you can learn quite a bit about your markets and gain a deep understanding of the current and predicted performance of your investments and competition. Insights from each of these pieces of information will help you develop a greater precision when sourcing deals of any kind—whether you're buying, selling, or servicing a property.

Depending on your area of expertise, different factors will be more relevant for you to gain a full picture of the market. Whatever the case, when undertaking your commercial real estate market analysis, follow my footsteps and hire a reputable expert with high-quality data sources. Thorough investigations, statistics, and figures, rather than opinion and speculation, should always support a strong commercial real estate analysis. To that end, here are items I learned after my first market analysis:

Obtain Market Reports. Sources as noted include market reports that provide an in-depth exploration of the latest trends in the commercial real estate sector, exploring assets and geographical location in detail. Market reports from industry leaders, such as CBRE, can provide you with confidence that your commercial real estate market analysis is informed by the expertise of specialists in the industry, who have access to superior sources of data.

Hire an Expert. To complement commercial real estate market analysis reports, I recommend that you hire an experienced consultant to assist you in your commercial real estate market analysis. It will make your life easy.

Find Property Values. This piece is what I spoke about and something you can gain expertise in. A key piece in any market is understanding the value of different asset types in your target market areas. You should also review the transactional history of properties, the previous year's assessed values of any property, as well as its most recent sale price.

Find Property Sales Volume. The national sales volume of markets across the nation is a factor for larger long-term investment. There are sources on recent sales volumes in markets and the most recent sale price in the last year to interpolate back to the previous year. These types of reports can give you full insight into the sales trends of a specific market.

Analyze Zoning and Regulations. Lastly, when looking at property data, you want to check zoning classifications attached to a property so your antenna is always up for top-down, forward outside the box thinking. This helps keep you up to date on master planning and possible double plays on properties that you first buy and stabilize based on existing conditions, and then you can capitalize a second time on the same property in a future development opportunity.

Residential Market Analysis

In case you haven't conducted or seen a residential comparative market analysis, don't sweat the small stuff. This is a task that drives itself because you asked the universe for the money, and the money drives the deal. It drove my assisted living project. Without the absorption issues addressed up front with the lender, you will not obtain debt financing. No lender will finance a commercial deal without their investment secured by a market analysis and values to support it. My team told me what I needed, and I listened. Residential analysis is an entirely different ball game.

If you were to walk into a real estate office today and ask them to help you buy a house listed in a particular market, they'd have a full report in less than twenty-four hours. That's what a real estate agent does to profit in the residential market. To perform a comparative market analysis for pure residential, your local Multiple Listing Service (MLS) will have real estate comps for the following:

1. Current Running Listings
2. Pending Listings
3. Sold Listings
4. Expired Listings

Typically, with the real estate agency being familiar with their territory, the concerning market items can be addressed off the cuff. However, if residential is your initial bailiwick, then you can certainly take this on as your own. Should you decide to do that, consider the following for a residential real estate market analysis:

Become Aware. Most large real estate brokers offer quarterly market reports that reflect the larger state of the market in terms of what's selling, for how much, and how fast. Homebuyers should immerse themselves in everything real estate in their targeted demographic. If you are in the market, you should consider meeting the contractor and the top-performing agents in that area. Consider market cues. If making a long-term investment, seek stable areas with good schools, multiple major employers, and moderate population growth. If short term, look for the hot areas where investors are improving value. Your short-term equity gains may far outpace appreciation.

Google It. A simple Internet search is the best place to start. You must be specific with your search terms. Something like zip code is a good place to start. Most likely, people you rely on for information did the same thing at some point.

Social Media and Community. It's important to look at local news, community websites, social media, and even bloggers in the area. These outlets can provide broader and different insights into the market than an agent, thanks to their unique perspective.

Understand Market Cycles. It is very important to know real estate market cycles.

- Study the building types you buy or sell.
- Understand comps in your market.
- Know variable improvement costs and minimum sales.
- Sell in a seller's market to achieve best price.
- Buy in a buyer's market to negotiate the best deal.
- The higher the risk, the higher the reward.

Do Your Research. If you want to buy in a specific neighborhood, immerse yourself in the area before you buy or select an agent. You can find data on one of the most popular websites, Zillow. We have found that their Zestimates are high. We conservatively use them as one of our sources to average property values before auction.

Turning Your Market Analysis into Action

Changing gears a bit, it is important to turn your market analysis into an action plan to secure the real estate transaction. The good news, regardless of your profession, is that there are several ways you can utilize this in the commercial real estate market analysis. No matter your role in your commercial real estate investment venture, possessing in-depth insight into the market will give you an edge and help you close a higher number of profitable deals. This type of action plan will eventually lead to networks and help you access off-market properties.

If you are a commercial real estate broker, I may be preaching to the choir since you are trained to always keep your finger on the heartbeat of the latest market trends. Further expertise, technological advances, and data-driven apps can provide you with a more informed picture of the market, allowing you to impress your prospects and clients with your knowledge of the market.

On the flip side (no pun intended) as a commercial real estate investor, staying on the radar about the latest local news and supply and demand trends can absolutely help you tap into very lucrative upside opportunities. Therefore, no matter your profession, commercial real estate market analysis can become a hobby if you have a passion for it. Through the use of new technology and artificial intelligence, it can also help you uncover new opportunities to foreshadow future complications and allow you to hone your expertise to generate ongoing business.

Technological Advancement in Our Business

When it comes to evaluating the market, it is crucial to understand the technological advances available to investors. Over the last few years, I've begun to see these advancements in my construction business. It started in 1992, when I saw the future and wrote a paper called

"Plan Room 2000." In that paper, I envisioned electronic plan rooms to eliminate the hundreds of thousands of dollars we were spending on drawing reproduction costs. I saw that it was a way of the future, and sure enough, twenty years later, it's the only thing we use now with a massive amount of project data at our fingertips.

Recently, a few of the items we are now using to embrace technology in lieu of resisting include:

Building Information Modeling (BIM). This uses 3D models to show what renderings look like as well as the inner workings of the mechanical and electrical systems. My team used this technology to coordinate our mechanical, electrical, and plumbing trades through multistory skyscrapers in New York City. We did this live online with participants located in different places throughout the country, an advancement that is a far different from the old days. In another era, we would overlay trade shop drawings on Mylar over the course of several weeks in different colors to see vertical and horizontal hits to be coordinated.

AR/VR Devices. Another item we used regularly at Flipping USA was augmented and virtual reality wearables and AR/VR devices that were a significant driver in the innovation of our sales process. AR/VR aided in the visualization of the properties firsthand where wholesale buyers could take a virtual tour inside the investment property to see the improvements that had to be complete. This allowed us to estimate cost remotely using this technology.

Internet-connected Sensors and Devices. Digitally optimized new construction modern-building management thrives on new construction as well as comprehensive renovations and innovative construction techniques. For that reason, Internet-connected sensors and devices have quickly become a competitive requirement for commercial real estate owners. On my project at 221 W 29th Street, we had the leaning tower of Pisa. The adjacent building begins to settle and moves in the westerly direction 8.1 inches. We were minutes away from evacuating the adjacent building. We took steps to inject high-strength grout beneath the footing and installed temporary rakers to support further movement. We also implemented a six-month plan to stop any further settlement, allowing us to continue erection of our new structure. To control this process, we installed digital survey sensors on the building across the street that monitored real time data and movement. It was an amazing process, however this one kept me up at night.

These are just a few of the opportunities available to us today. They are only the tip of the iceberg. I'm excited to begin using the new technologies and applications in the real estate industry. Our challenge in the construction industry is often felt through the resistance of others, especially when technology can improve the environment yet ends up not being implemented. Typically, it takes the attention of the owner to see the added value of the new technologies and applications. But this technology is coming our way and becoming the industry norm, whether we move toward these trends or not.

A Glimpse into the Future

Technological advancement can affect everything in the world. It used to be that game-changing innovations came only once in a lifetime. However, with blockchain technology and artificial intelligence entering the limelight, things are changing at a rapid pace.

I believe we will begin to see our world disrupted on an almost daily basis with new technology. Changes that used to occur over several generations now happen in a decade or less. This is true across the globe and in every industry. No one is safe. And if the rapid rise of social networking has taught us anything, it's that the real estate industry is going to change as well. Artificial intelligence is one of the biggest new technologies of the twenty-first century. This is the process by which computers are imbued with the ability to "think" like an intelligent being.

Until now, we've seen minimal reaction from the real estate and construction industries, even though real estate and construction will have a profound impact as in any other industry. Are we ready for this further advancement in technology that will require almost everyone to adapt the way they live, work, and consume? We might ask this because of speculation at this time. What drivers and trends will decisively impact the future of real estate investing so you can remain successful moving forward?

As an investor, you can stay ahead of the curve by implementing new technologies and acclimating to change in the market and real estate environment with effective strategies to meet the demands of tomorrow.

From faster, more accurate appraisals to sophisticated forecasts, the use of analytics can lead to smarter decisions about property investments. Considering all the data that real estate and its users generate, it seems likely that companies specializing in big data processing will enter the real estate services market.

Another concept that seems to be taking the industry by storm is the way in which people work. You may have heard of the recent WeWork mission, which is to *Create a world where people work to make a life, not only a living.* This approach has sent companies into transformation mode toward ever-increasing requirements around flexibility and space optimization. Thanks to new technologies that make a flexible, variable workplace relocation technically possible, and even socially appealing, this development has once again picked up speed.

The Deloitte Global study "Global Human Capital Trends 2018" outlines disruptive changes that demand efficient flexibility and radical innovation from companies. In today's networked organizations, a combination of technology, physical space design, new leadership approaches, and new work practices must all come together to achieve this goal. This requires collaboration among company divisions and the commitment to build an integrated, customized work environment. The downtown Manhattan Amazon integrated office is an example of a free environment where if you have an account with Amazon then you can use the office space. It is really cool!

Combination to the Safe

My take on all this is that "data" is the combination that opens your business to consistent opportunity. After reading the book *The*

Formula a few years back, I learned that data could absolutely predict results. Then I looked at the uses of data in real estate, a fascinating endeavor. I was unaware of the extent that data was being used to find deals at my level. I just thought it was kind of a word of mouth thing as a player in the game. But little did I know that a whole new world in data advancements would revolutionize real estate.

What did I find? Artificial Intelligence (AI) and Machine Learning (ML) for real estate. These ML software tools recognize patterns in data that humans cannot derive. They then use these patterns to generate insights for decision-making. For instance, it can indicate future market trends, property types that will profit in the future, and predictable results around your business strategies and plan.

AI systems can scan massive amounts of data patterns from historical sales records to identify demand on certain market types. This information can help real estate investors, developers, marketers, salespeople, and brokers on their strategies to capitalize on opportunities.

If you compare current appraisal techniques discussed herein, often based on listings and sale prices, they fail to consider major factors related to value like transportation and infrastructure improvements, environmental impact, local master plans, and other amenities (like schools, stores, and proximity to public transportation) that all impact the value of the property. Because of pattern recognition abilities, ML software can be of great assistance in resolving major unknowns by revealing the numerous value factors.

Another advantage of AI is personal productivity and the elimination of repetitive tasks that may require human intelligence, which relieves demand on our most costly commodity—time.[3] This in turn will allow professionals to focus on tasks that deliver the biggest bang for the buck. Here's my takeaway from the book *Getting Things Done*: The mind is not designed to remember, it's designed to create. So why not surrender to your new personal assistant?

With all eyes on artificial intelligence and machine learning, it's clear that with this technology, along with blockchain technology, we are in for a bit of a ride and an acclimation period due to their major impact on the future of real estate—the ability to offer liquidation in real estate and to collect, analyze, and learn from data to eliminate uncertainty.

With these new exciting advancements in our ability to conduct a real estate market analysis, it brings even more excitement to the next chapter, "Money, Money, Money."

Money is a terrible master but an excellent servant.

P.T. Barnum, *entertainer and entrepreneur*

CHAPTER 6

MONEY, MONEY, MONEY:
Creating Unlimited Funding for
Diversified Real Estate Transactions

"Show me the money!"

Being a former athlete and sports movie enthusiast, I absolutely love that famous line from the movie *Jerry Maguire*. But you have to wonder, as Jerry was yelling out the phrase, was he actually valuing the money or treating it as if it were his own? A key to fundraising is treating the almighty dollar as if it's your own because money is the Holy Grail of real estate. Without it or the mindset to find it, you are cooked before you even step into the batter's box. That being said, let me show you the money so you can position yourself to raise unlimited funds for your real estate investment deals.

When did the value of money hit home for you? It was long before my dad told me to get a job and I started hustling every day on my paper route at age twelve, waking up daily at 5 a.m. to drop the *Star Ledger* at neighbors' homes. I would load those fifty-plus newspapers into a canvas bag that I would then jury-rig onto my bicycle handlebars. And off I went. Home by 6:30, I was ready to shower and start my day in preparation for school and sports in the evening at Donaldson Park.

It was a good start, but not nearly enough opportunity. So I then started my magic business in hopes of making more money. You may have grown up in a wealthy family where the value of money was discussed at the dinner table, but my household was a bit different. We absolutely struggled to survive. My dad worked two jobs till nine p.m. Mom worked all day, and Grandma took care of us. It wasn't easy at all. With just a few dollars in my pocket, I scraped together enough to buy magic tricks to support my new business performing at children's birthday parties. With that, the journey began.

So how does this value of the money relate to real estate? Well, there a few things I want you to consider. Even though there are instances where you can buy real estate with no money down, it's much easier when you have working capital to maneuver while you are also teeing up deals to place investors' money.

So how do you beg, borrow, and get creative regardless of your circumstances? You may even be curious about what type of money it takes to invest in the various types of real estate that we discussed earlier. How much do I need to get started in residential? How much do I need to get started in commercial? How much do I need to get my first deal? If you are like me, these are just a few of the questions running through your head. If you could only imagine the number of sleepless nights I experienced trying to figure out real estate investing and how I would support twins.

Let's face it, the mechanics of real estate are not rocket science. But you do have to map out this money thing relative to what you can do without having to go overboard with a financial plan on how to execute with small, medium, or large amounts of money. The main factor is your presence to and understanding of funding projects. After that, we can look at the cash position relative to your current lifestyle to see if your strategy correlates to the path that resonates with you.

Establishing some parameters for this discussion, it is important to note that having no money doesn't necessarily mean you have zero dollars at your disposal. It just means you are relatively stable, the lights are on, and you don't have equity to contribute to an investment. We will define small money as $25,000 to $100,000 in working capital, medium money as $100,000 to $1 million in capital, and big money as $1 million or more.

With that said, it is important to better understand where your money can go in these deals. Here is an example to identify the itemization of the expenditures you'll need to buy an investment property. Imagine you were buying a fix and flip and then looking to maintain the investment property. The following are the items with cost parameters that should be included in your assumptions:

Due Diligence. For residential properties, this includes home, termite, radon, chimney, and oil tank inspections. These costs are usually around $1,000 to $1,500.

Closing Costs. Generally, these are 3.5 percent of the purchase price and include costs to pay for title company fees, lender fees, loan escrows, first-year insurance, a property inspection, and the deed preparation fees.

Improvement Costs. Your improvements to your investment can make it or break it, so it is important to understand the concept of Guaranteed Maximum Price (GMP), which is the maximum price guaranteed by the contractor. The GMP must include repair budget items like bath and kitchen upgrades, windows, roofing, new services, and pretty much anything else required to create a WOW factor when they walk in the door, make it livable, and provide nice finishes.

Interest. These are payments to the lender typically made during the improvement period. However, our residential lender in New Jersey, Peak Properties, has a program that allows you to finance without paying interest until you close. It's very attractive even though the rates are typically as much as 12 percent to 14 percent. If you don't have a choice, this option will work.

Carry Costs. During the improvement period and thereafter, you have to carry holding costs like a mortgage payment, property insurance, taxes, and utilities for a few months while you're fixing it up and finding a new tenant.

Maintenance Costs. This is not applicable in our previous example, but it is a must for your buy and holds and would include costs you pay each year like lawn care, snow removal, gutters, and larger things over time like window and roof replacement, siding, driveway repair, landscape update, etc.

Reserves. If you have six months of mortgage payments and credit card leverage reserved, it would be ideal. This is my rule of thumb for estimating reserves along with calculating the reserves on a property-by-property basis. Therefore, you can estimate how much you'll need set aside for the comfort level to jump in.

It is important to fluently learn these cost itemizations, as they give you the innate ability to compute opportunities on the spot and negotiate like an all-star. However, this chapter is really about how much money you have and how to best invest it. To help you better understand this, I created the ballpark levels of money to see where you stand in the lineup, how your initial strategy applies to executing your game plan, and the bottom line on what it takes for you to hit a home run.

Ballpark Levels of Money

Water Boy – Little or No Money

Yes, I was at the status of water boy not long ago. However, I quickly learned that this journey was through the desert with a team of experts, and I was the most important guy in the bunch. I was close enough to get a taste of the Gatorade. So, if you are tapped like I was, you need to get very creative to find the money. Let's assume you have money to stay afloat, you are working, have a few bucks saved, or you're in the business and in between deals, waiting for a closing.

It's hard to convince someone to invest with you when you have no money or stability. You don't need your own place necessarily; however, you need to be in a relatively sustainable position on a month-to-month basis. And there are exceptions to the rules if you are hungry enough. However, you must toughen up and stay focused on your plan and mission. It's helpful if you have a few extra dollars to essentially dress impressive, find the equipment you need, and find a small office. If you are just getting started and have zero money, let me give you some things you can do for free too.

Get Educated. Start off by spending some time on Google researching real estate topics that come to mind. Then, look at the best locations, price ranges, and investment parameters, start a new note-book of important discoveries, and bookmark articles for future reading. Create your own curriculum in real estate, study markets, learn valuation details, investigate construction costs, find out the master development plans of towns near you, and realize the beauty of the Internet in helping with clarity and direction in your journey.

Explore Investment Options and Set Your Goals. Remember, people don't plan to fail, they fail to plan. And how would you expect to hit a target when you are unsure where you are to aim? Whatever you want to call it, goal or outcome, you need to have a purpose behind it.

The Cheapest Option. I think REITs are your cheapest and easiest option if you want to add real estate to your portfolio. You can own real estate today with these securities being traded on the major exchanges. You can get in for $5,000 if you are an accredited investor, and then you collect dividends with minimal control as discussed.

Leadoff Batter – $25,000 - $100,000

The leadoff spot is a unique position in the lineup, as it signifies an ability and unique skill set. Typically, leadoff batters are fast and have an above-average batting ability. Remember, the goal of the leadoff batter is to get on base. Leadoff batters in real estate are anxious to get rolling and are absolutely above average. Why? Because everyone and their brother would be doing it if this were easy. They know the value of money and have a few hard-earned dollars to show for it.

Great leadoff batters take a step back to ensure that they address all the foundational items to build upon. Since they are not necessarily dug in too deep as the leadoff, they have the luxury of time to prepare for bigger opportunities. Everything you need to rapidly proceed is here, enabling you to start off a winning lineup

But you are in the driver's seat as the leadoff batter and have some money to invest.

Moving up the Lineup – $100,000 - $1,000,000

I consider this a versatile position, as you can hit in several spots in the lineup. For example, you can be a great support for the cleanup hitter with a respectful on base percentage, or you can get it going in spots five to eight where you keep the momentum going. You're ready to go with lineup variety, but something is missing. Nothing is wrong, but you may be in this exact position of opportunity with a slight blind spot, not seeing what's missing in getting started or in your existing real estate business. It may be money, the ability to find deals, or figuring out how to pull off the execution of multiple deals while maintaining deal flow.

So it's much easier to get started for those investors that are open to learning from others and seek mentorship. You can start with further educating and aligning yourself with trusted advisors. You may want to passively dabble during your first deal and then target taking on your own. The next step may be an ideal syndication, where you bring a group of investors together to facilitate for a fee and ownership, with all investors meeting their financial goals. The sky's the limit.

Batting Cleanup - $1,000,000 and Up

Are you a clean-up hitter?

Being a New York Yankees fan, Babe Ruth (The Babe) comes to mind. Henry Aaron does as well. I'll never forget the night Aaron hit one out of the ballpark to break Babe Ruth's record. He was a powerful yet intelligent batter. You have to act in the same way and be smart so you don't get knocked down in the lineup let alone thrown out of the league because of a major financial hit. If you are serious about this thing and batting cleanup, team up with someone like myself so you have a kind of insurance policy to reduce risk, increase awareness to prevent pitfalls, and accelerate results.

Funding the Investment

At the end of the day, it is all about showing me the money. This is also known as funding the investment. Even though we have previously touched upon this, I would like to take a deeper dive into the various ways you can FUND real estate investments. This will help you determine exactly how you are going to procure the money and where you plan to put it. The more money you have, the greater the opportunity at your fingertips. Here are a few techniques that worked for me with no money when getting started:

Form Partnerships for Equity. Real estate partnerships are common for investing in real estate with little or no money. I did something interesting where I formed a subsidiary to my parent development company with twelve investment positions at $10,000/per. Each investor contributed smaller amounts of money for the first right of refusal to these investments.

Find the Down Payment. Like a partnership, find one nice person who will spot you the down payments so you can buy. Any ambitious person would give this method a try. And, if you don't ask, you will not receive the funds.

Seller Financing. This is one of the oldest and most proven ways to invest in real estate with no money. The seller holds the mortgage where you capitalize, subject to you fulfilling your monthly payment obligation without having to stress credit and cash available to buy the property until you improve your cash position.

Hard Money Lenders. The tough guys usually want your firstborn. However, when you don't have a choice, hard money is perfect to fund your investments.

Home Equity Loans. This is a credit line secured by your personal residence.

State and Government Loans. This worked for me extremely well on my first project financed by the New Jersey Economic Development Agency (NJEDA). It was a municipal bond vehicle facilitated through the NJEDA platform where municipal bonds were sold to municipalities for a projected rate of return, which resulted in $17 million toward my first development! And I had no clue at first, until my resourcefulness, research, and due diligence found that the money was available.

In addition to these unique mechanisms available to you as an investor, let's look at the many finance options in greater detail because they will apply to all levels of money on the playing field.

Debt Loan Options

The American people are aware that banks have been the main source of funds for buying real estate, especially after the depression and the market adjustment we all experienced in 2008 with the savings and loan crisis. After that incident, financial institutions were regulated and are now monitored on their standards and performance. With that said, let's look deeper at the source of loans available to assist you in building your empire. The typical loan we all know about is the one used to purchase a home as a homeowner. This is a conventional loan from a bank that has either a fixed or adjustable rate known as a mortgage.

Fixed Rate Conventional Loan. Both fixed and adjustable rate mortgages are a good solution for investors building a portfolio of rental properties and not an option to wholesale and flip houses.

Pros
- Easy to understand and qualify
- Competitive market interest rates
- No principal mortgage insurance (PMI) if you put 20 percent down

Cons
- You need a good credit score
- Limitation on the quantity of loans
- Not available to partnerships
- You can't compete with cash buyers
- Nonrefundable loan origination fees

Adjustable-Rate Conventional Mortgage (ARM). An adjustable-rate mortgage is exactly what it says, a loan that has a rate adjustable with market fluctuation.

Pros
- Lower initial interest rates than fixed mortgages
- Thought that your interest rate will adjust downward
- Ideal for short-term finance

Cons
- Rates increasing above fixed rates
- Unreliable prediction of your average interest rate
- Amortization is not easy to understand

Federal Housing Authority (FHA) Loans. These types of loan require qualification relative to income as they are government-sponsored to incentivize people to purchase a home.

Pros
- Low down payment estimate at 3.5 percent
- Easier to qualify with credit score

Cons
- You must live in the house
- Higher PMI tradeoff for the lower-rate loan
- Limited to ONLY one FHA loan at a time and a lot of paperwork
- Strict appraisal needed for approval

Veteran Affairs (VA) Loan. The VA loan is one of the great advantages of serving our country, a benefit I fully support knowing what my son does as a US Marine. This loan offers our service members the opportunity to buy a home with no down payment.

Pros
- No down payment
- Very low interest rates available
- No required PMI
- Lower closing costs
- Not limited to one property

- Higher allowable debt-to-income ratio
- You can effectively build a portfolio

Cons
- Limited access
- You must live in the property for one year
- Much more paperwork at application and closing

203(k) Loan. This loan is like an FHA loan in the context of structure, but it should only be used if you are buying a fixer-upper with a plan to call it your home. The unique selling point of this loan, in addition to the pros of the FHA loan, is that you can lump the improvement costs into the mortgage and there is no need for a future takeout of high-interest money.

Pros
- Only one lender required
- Can include distressed and foreclosed properties
- Greater equity potential
- Approval of self-performed rehab work to lower cost
- Includes the rehab costs in loan

Cons
- Available only to owner occupants
- Self-performed work will have to be supported with paperwork from a licensed contractor
- Contractors must be approved by your lender
- Much paperwork like VA and FHA loans

Private Money Loan. Private money is exactly as described, private, typically from individuals in lieu of family office and institutional investors.

Pros
- Fewer qualifications are needed
- Very flexible loan structure, Fast closings
- Flexibility in loan terms
- No underwriting hassle
- Attractive interest rates

- Unlimited number of deal volume
- Not using personal credit
- Ability to fund deals banks won't

Cons

- Higher interest rates
- Legal counsel required
- Short term
- Riskier with short-term and higher interest rates

Hard Money. Hard money is like private money, but the difference is the source. Instead of coming from an individual, the funding comes from a hard money lender. The term "hard money" is fitting, because the lenders use the hard asset (the property) to secure the loan.

Pros

- Very flexible structure
- Easy to qualify for because the loan is secured by the property rather than your personal financials
- Very quick turnaround from application to funding
- Hard money loans are easy to find

Cons

- Higher interest rate than other loans: 10 to 12%
- Higher closing costs
- Shorter terms

Home Equity Line of Credit (HELOC). The home equity line of credit is also known as a HELOC. This is money that homeowners can use if they have equity. They can use this money as a loan to buy other properties.

Pros

- Controllable
- Inexpensive
- No prepayment penalty
- Lower closing costs
- Lower interest rates
- Most flexible type of financing

- Allows wealth leverage

Cons
- Increases your personal debt
- Lowers your net worth
- No control on the market interest rates

The Bottom Line

Taking all this into consideration and based on different options just mentioned, assumptions, and estimated costs to buy an investment property, we should identify the types of loans or costs of money that would be ideal but not required. This will get us to the bottom line, so if you don't have it, you are going to figure out how to find the money using the Modern Wealth Building Formula.

Here is an example of how the money conversation plays out in the real world. Let's look at an investment property with an acquisition cost of $100,000, estimated improvement costs of $50,000, and a six-month turnaround with an after repair value (ARV) of $275,000. What money would you need to buy it? To fix it? To sell it for a profit in six months? My rule of thumb is that you should target $10,000 per month in minimum profit, which would equal a $60,000 target profit over the period of this deal. Here are how the numbers look:

Due Diligence	$1,500	
Acquisition Cost	$100,000	
Improvement Costs	$50,000	
Closing Costs	$3,500	
Interest	$9,600	Estimate 2% to close plus 12% on total for six months
Carry Costs	$6,000	Assume $1,000/month
Subtotal:	**$169,000**	
Contingency	$8,460	5%
Total Est. Cost:	**$177,660**	Conservatively round up to $180,000

Make Sure to Be Conservative. It's much better to overpromise and underdeliver your finished masterpiece. Based on this paper napkin analysis, this is what a typical deal might look like once you factor in all the money. With hard money lenders generally requiring 80 percent of the purchase price and 90 percent of improvement costs, for a quick calculation we figure 20 percent equity (down payment required) on the total estimated cost. So, on this investment, a 20 percent deposit on your first deal until you establish credibility, we would be looking at equity in the amount of $36,000 and debt of $144,000 to make the deal happen.

Now that you have the ballpark dollar amount, if you want to effortlessly obtain deals like this I would suggest you take $75,000 to $100,000 in working capital to churn two of these out per year without a glitch. If you prefer an orchestra to a one-man band, then you should inquire about the next level. The next level considers the different buying tiers of pure residential being low, $10,000 to $250,000, medium, $250,000 to $500,000, and high, $500,000 and above.

If you don't have the cash on hand right now, then take whatever action you can until you do. That might be getting a raise or second job, lowering your own housing costs and living expenses, or selling that second car you don't need. Your financial future isn't going to just happen on its own. It's going to take some sacrifices and massive action on your part.

Unlimited Funding

By now you must be thinking, *How is it possible to have unlimited funding?* One thing I thought of was while I was drilling deep and three feet from gold is that it always sounded like a good catch. Yes, I was able to raise $100,000 on my first go-around. But we all know it's impossible to catch a unicorn. Until a few years ago, I couldn't even fathom the possibility of unlimited funding.

In general, three simple tips will unlock the door to unlimited funding. Trust me when I say that these three tips will keep your investors returning round after round, which allows them to be your *"go to"* source for unlimited funding. If you can master these tips and provide consistent ROI, you will have access to more money than you could have ever imagined. With that said, here you go:

Tip #1: Buy Below Market Value. Know the market by following my recommendations on market analysis and find out the median price of your chosen market type properties in your targeted areas. A realtor, Zillow, or quick Google search can tell you the ballpark market value.

Tip #2: Do Your Homework. Don't expect anyone to take you seriously if you don't do your homework. Like anything, you become an expert after putting in the time and money to understand the market and the investment and to craft a strong strategy.

Tip #3: Negotiate Your Ass Off. To maximize an outcome on your investment, it starts by getting the best price, which means making a smaller deposit and recognizing a greater rate of return. So don't take this lightly. This can make or break a long-term reputation, relationships, and it only goes one way. Be prepared to walk away. There are no square pegs that fit in a round hole, so don't let your emotional attachment hook you into a loser. On the other hand, people forget that investment prices aren't set in stone. Regardless, if you're in a very hot market, it never hurts to make a lower offer. In either event, you must be fully prepared with your numbers to negotiate effectively. Trust that your competition will be prepared and will not accept any gut offers to pay less. If owners are unwilling to consider your offer, hold off on purchasing unless the numbers work at the sale price. Or you can always touch base with them every couple of weeks to see if they're willing to come back to the bargaining table.

Remember, real estate had an average annual return of 11.42 percent since 1970 compared to the S&P 500 that has an average of an annual return of 10.31 percent. With the upside potential being much higher in real estate, and the sheer fact that you have more control, you would be mistaken if you did not take advantage of real estate appreciating faster, generating more cash flow, and being less affected by downturn markets.

I can hear you saying, "Did you really have to remind me about negotiation and the art of the deal?" I'm good. Just tell me what unlimited funding looks like. Before we go there, let's look at critical viewpoints relative to private lenders. These viewpoints will help you around private lending where you might be asking, "What does a private investor look for, and how can I find them?"

From my experience, private lenders know what they want, what to look for, and find these to be the primary items to open this coffer:
- Good Reporting and Communication
- Secured Capital
- Consistent Returns
- Passive Income
- Presentable Documentation

You are going to be extremely surprised when you find out how many private lenders are out there. I'll even bet there is one in your circle of influence that you haven't even thought of yet. In the old days without the Internet, meet-up groups, and networking events, it could take weeks if not months to pitch numerous investors. But nowadays, it's instantaneous and accessible. However, there is a difference in Internet contacts versus the old-fashioned way, networking and generating business contacts face-to-face, which has always been a key to success. If you recall the Smith Barney TV commercial with the perspective "We make money the old-fashioned way," here are some vehicles to find private lenders:

- Real Estate Clubs
- Real Estate Seminars
- Mortgage Brokers
- Real Estate Agents
- Internet Real Estate Forums
- Referrals
- Public Records

Each of these can offer great opportunity to network and find similarly minded people that are interested in investing and making money. But even then, the market is constantly in flux. Deals and money are here today and gone tomorrow. You have to move quickly, remain flexible like a shortstop, and be ready for the ball to come your way.

Changing the Lineup: The Future of Funding

All great coaches alternate and move players around in the lineup to match the changing environment of the game, which you must recognize in real estate. You are setting yourself up for failure when you keep a right-handed pitcher in the game against a right-handed batter. A simple adjustment can often make all the difference in the win and loss column. What is the difference of the look of a curveball thrown by a right-hander versus a lefty when you relate that question to real estate? You might ask, "What does unlimited funding look like?" It looks like freedom to do what you want, when you want, and how you want. One thing is certain, funding is always available for quality real estate.

When it comes to the importance of "unlimited," it's ideal to establish relationships across the gamut of private investors to institutions to securitize funds. As you are most likely aware, in my opinion, banks will no longer be the main source of funding. Due to severe competition, recovery challenges, and regulations enforced after the savings and loan crisis, we have seen that there is a whole new space for less traditional funding sources with different structure and lending terms and flexibility with vertically integrated companies. In my opinion, even though there are currently unlimited bank sources, many of the newbies in the finance world will increase market share substantially.

These new capital sources have now and will continue to become common in real estate finance. As you learn, these options are a means to unlimited funding because they are a vertically integrated process. They will consist of a combination of high-net individuals, family offices, and institutions. When used for development, these capital sources may include additional parameters and benchmarks. They also have higher interest rates in many cases. Based on these factors, banks may acclimate with other less traditional lenders with higher costs taking business from them. Let's see how it all plays out.

You will see securitization of real estate increase with the advancement in technology, globalization, and tokenization. We are seeing them in more specialized areas than we once did. Now, they are necessary evils to attract funding from a variety of sources with many targeting the opportunity zones. This will level the playing field for smaller investors, and due to the continuous rumblings on Wall Street and my prediction of the exodus of large sums of money from the stock market, it will also lead to the extraction of baby boomer money as they retire and more move toward less risky investments. Wall Street and large bank financial institutions will make a move to retain funds in the securitized platforms by introducing more securitized funding through banks limited due to regulations, so money may be more difficult to obtain from this source.

Since the main objective of financial institutions is to reduce risk and make sure people have skin in the game, they now shy away and ensure that they are not on the hook for 100 percent of the financing of any project. Thus, it leads you to use the Modern Wealth Building Formula to get creative and adapt to the changes in the lineup. In all cases, the training in this book, practical experience, integrity, and commitment to continuous and never-ending improvement (CANI) of your skill sets will be extremely important in any space of the real estate you choose.

LUCK is PREPARATION meeting OPPORTUNITY! Precise use of the formula and ensuring you follow the steps to the T, focused on every detail with no shortcuts, will be the part of formula to assist you with getting unlimited funding.

If you were worried before reading this chapter about not having cash to buy an investment property, then don't sweat it. I was in the same boat. Luckily, I've outlined for you the techniques I used to get started, as well as numerous sources of equity and debt finance options. They are literally everywhere. Funding is right in front of your eyes. There are numerous sources of funding both on equity and debt sides of the fence. What I've found is that the money will come as you invest the time and energy into making the right decision. Remember the field of dreams? If you build it then they shall come. I truly believe this because when I started, I had nothing to show. It was extremely challenging and I was severely scrutinized; however with steady determination and drive, we were able to obtain the funding.

The Winning Lineup

Money, money, money is the most important part of any real estate investment process. However, building a great team is a close second. With a strong leadoff batter, cleanup hitter, and anything and everything in between, your talent will make your money go even further than it could on its own. When the principals are aligned and come together, money just flows into your bank account. It's like being at a casino on the Atlantic City Boardwalk playing a slot machine and hitting the jackpot. The earnings just flow into your hands.

For me, it all started with my first workup of a deal that I would see rinsed and repeated numerous times over. I was not sure how to do it at the time. But looking back now, I ask myself what step-by-step process I took to be successful both on and off the field. To that end, here is the batting order for the winning lineup to see a return on your next deal:

1. Shift Your Mindset and Belief System
2. Get Clear on Your Goals and Vision
3. Create Real Estate Investing and Wealth Plans
4. Understand the "FIND" Protocol to Secure Profitable Deals
5. Master the Art of Negotiating Deals
6. Become an Expert in the "FUND" Process
7. Generate Fee Gold and Scale Your Business
8. Ace the "FACILITATE" Process
9. Engage in Personal Development and Performance Training

A great starting lineup can be an extremely effective way to reach your goals and succeed in real estate investing. You are only as good as the money you have and the team you put into place to support it. Even one out-of-position team member can create a tremendous gap in your lineup that might impact the entire performance of your portfolio. So while the subject of this chapter is "Show me the money," the reality is that you need more than just some coin to really hit it big in the real estate market. In fact, a poorly structured or organized team can cost you all your funding anyway. Good batting isn't as nearly as effective if you don't have great pitching to support it. The same is true in real estate.

Money + Great Team + Thoughtful Organization = True Success

And that is what I want for you and your real estate portfolio. The best part is that the relationship is cyclical. The better team you have, the more money people will entrust to you. And the more money you have, the greater your team can leverage this into meaningful investments. That is where the real magic happens.

The individual investor should act consistently as an investor and not as a speculator.

Benjamin Graham, *professor and economist*

CHAPTER 7

READY, SET, BUILD:
Starting Your Own Real Estate Investment Company

Is real estate investing the beauty or the beast? I would have to say you get the best of both worlds. It has the upside to be a beast of a win, and, in my view, it's an absolute beauty. The beauty of building a real estate business is like watching a sunrise—the entire horizon lights up in style.

You may recall my grammar school class trip to New York City. It was amazing to look at these remarkable architectural masterpieces. Coming back from the city, I knew right then and there that my dream was to build a skyscraper. Just the view alone was indescribable at the time. But even then, I couldn't appreciate all that these buildings had to offer. However, today I now see the amazing results of being in the business of real estate. It has been a true beauty, and I haven't once looked back.

I never would have imagined being where I am today. In some ways I am taking a stroll down memory lane in writing this book, looking back at how this all came to fruition. It's a bit of a blur now, and many years have passed since that first glance at the towering structures.

This singular recollection from 1980 planted a seed in my soul. Shortly after high school graduation, I read a newly published book on buying real estate with no money down. Robert Allen, who wrote this book, eventually became a friend. It was an honor to meet the man who sent me on a mission to figure out how to buy big-time real estate with no money down.

When you don't have money and you want real estate, you only have one choice—it's called work with what you've got. I couldn't even fathom how someone could buy real estate, a physical house, with no money down. How could that be? It costs money to buy a car, food, and clothes. How could someone buy a house with no money?

After a depressing start at Rowen University (formerly Glassboro State) and a first year 1.6 GPA, I didn't think I would ever become an engineer. I failed both calculus and physics because my priorities were in chasing women and drinking beer. After three years of playing college football and partying my ass off in a pre-engineering program, I transferred to the New Jersey Institute of Technology to focus on engineering and finally completed a four-year degree on the six-year plan. It was my proud accomplishment to have matured into an honor roll graduate.

After graduating, I started a job as an engineer, sitting at a desk all day and designing development sites. Shortly thereafter, I started my career at Lehrer McGovern Bovis, a well-respected worldwide construction firm. I remained there until 1996, before I developed for RHR Holdings, Aby Rosen on 64th Street, Bruce Eichner on 80th Street, and then became a partner in a general contracting company before venturing out on my own. This led me to the notion that I might be able to successfully start my own business. But I wasn't thinking about real estate at the time. I was focusing on construction management and becoming the king of the hill in another company.

When I joined the GC firm, they were performing about $5 million in volume per year. But after bringing in my systems to revamp their many protocols, in less than one year from my onboarding we were doing over $40 million per year. I then came to find that the majority owner wanted to build a minority women's business-owned entity focused on minority work to promote his daughter, a rising star in the PWC, Professional Women in Construction. This wasn't my area of expertise. I wanted to take them into full skyscraper mode, but they had another agenda.

Thus, in 1998, I decided to part ways and take the leap into starting my own real estate business. There was some "faithing" it until you make it, giving presentation after presentation with no meat since I literally had no experience. But I just kept collecting samples of presentations and trucked along while hitting roadblocks. I formed my own entity, and it must have been the fertilizer to germinate the seeds of buying real estate with no money. It was a tenuous experience, but I was serious about building my company and investing. However, I knew that developing was the epicenter of real estate investing, allowing me to capitalize on the opportunity to generate fees for providing services. The rest is history. Now, over twenty years later, we are doing project after project, building monumental structures that kiss the clouds. I couldn't be happier.

To that end, have you ever thought about your vision for your real estate investment company? Ever considered how it would look if you started your own company or expanded your existing business? Will you eventually have an investment company you can call your own? Think about it for a second.

I took one year to sort and mastermind my next move. But then in 1999, my mother in-law (who rarely talked to me), called me out of the blue to mention that her boss's country club was having an outing to recruit new members. Knowing that I could not afford a country club membership, I figured I could at least get a free round of golf, a nice lunch, and not feel guilty about coming to the table with no intention of actually joining.

As I played the first hole, I daydreamed about joining a country club. That would be cool. I would be around people that had money that might invest in my real estate developments once they heard about them. Sounded easy! By the end of the round, I wanted to figure out this whole country club thing because of this crazy thought that I could raise money from other members. I still had no experience or clue how I was going to buy land or develop real estate with no money. And the pressure was building to figure out a way to generate income.

Believe it or not, there was an executive special to join the country club. For just $5,000, the club would waive the initiation fee and bond. Clearly, they were desperate to get members. I went home and begged my wife to allow me to charge a credit card so that I could follow my dream.

Still on the job, I started to play golf on weekends, away from my wife and twins for six-hour clips. This didn't help my work/life balance at all. A few days into my membership and my third round on the course, I was playing with a young hotshot who told me about his own success story. He was making a boatload of money. By the fourth hole, I wanted to tell him my story. I was as ready as I would ever be, so I figured I would give it a shot. I had nothing to lose. All he could say was NO.

I told him my story, and he asked if he could be a partner in my business. I was taken aback at how easy it was to find some coin. He committed $100,000 toward KJV Development by the end of the round. I had no money to invest or experience in raising money and once again, I forged ahead to figure out how to succeed. I proceeded with confidence to raise $1.6 million toward my first $17 million real estate development. It was then that I was off to the races on something that was all my own.

It's MINE

What is it like to have something you can call your own? I can tell you it is an absolutely   amazing feeling. No matter how many deals I complete, I still feel like each deal has the same glory and joy of my first. Having your own business is a remarkable endeavor, filled with tremendous ups and downs. But in the end, you enjoy the benefits of all your hard work. There I was, something all my own. It may sound selfish, however it strengthened my heart to help others.

I knew that more millionaires become millionaires in real estate, but do you know that more millionaires have earned their first million from real estate development than from any other industry out there? While true, being a real estate developer is one of the highest-risk businesses to begin with. It is probably safe to say that most first-time developers fail to make significant profit because they lack planning and are unaware of the pitfalls. However, opening a real estate development company is worth every minute of your time because the sky's the limit and the benefits are contagious.

Even more so, there is great opportunity in creating a real estate development company. Initially, you might wonder what a real estate development and investment company does and what are its benefits. In short, a real estate developer (also referred to as a sponsor) handles the project from beginning to end. It's the entity that buys the property, obtains entitlement to development, improves the land with the addition of structures that house residents or businesses, and eventually sells or rents out the building or space to third parties.

Normally, the developer is much like an orchestra leader, ensuring that all parties are working together. The developer will arrange a large group of professionals that will perform the various professional tasks necessary for the development to succeed. So next time you see an office building, shopping malls, landmarked estates, skyscrapers, or any other development, know that they are the work of real estate developers.

There are so many benefits to running your own real estate investment company. To start, you don't answer directly to anyone. You have mentors available for assistance instead of a one-way boss, and you can engage in accountability partners to ensure that you stay on track. And you can go golfing when you want.

For me, I realized my experience in construction was only one of the necessary skills to be a great developer. With this realization, I knew that mastering these skills was going to be the lead-in to my success. If I had already mastered the highest risk portion of the development—constructing the building—I knew I could succeed if I could learn how to mitigate the risk around raising money and avoidable pitfalls.

So why do people become involved in real estate developments? Because it is one of the most leveraged businesses possible, capable of generating profits and remarkable results if the plan goes right. With my teachings, you can minimize risks to create an effective plan that considers all the variables necessary to succeed. If I were to itemize the benefits of owning your own real estate company, I would include, at minimum, things like cash flow, tax breaks, appreciation, and control.

Some additional benefits might include:

- More Control of Your Destiny
- Ability to Earn Fees
- Underwriting Influence
- Additional Cash Flow
- Freedom of Running Your Own Investments
- Improving Your City/Town
- Creating Jobs

Any one of these benefits likely sounds pretty amazing on its own. But think about how you'd feel if you had the opportunity to combine additional cash flow, freedom, and the ability to come and go as you please. The sky is literally the limit. That is in part what makes real estate investing so special—it can offer you many different iterations of the same remarkable story.

Ready, Set, Build

Did I mention that my son is a sharpshooter? He achieved this status in his first year of officer training at Quantico. When talking about the discipline of this training, he said, "Dad, you can't even believe the accuracy of the sharpshooters that go on to be snipers. They train and have accuracy with precision to hit somebody with a bullet between the eyes at 2,000 feet away."

So I'm sure you've heard of ready, aim, shoot. If so, I bet you have found, just like me, that sometimes you take this in the wrong order. During the early part of my career, I was shooting all over the place trying to hit an eventual development goal without being prepared. I was ensuring that the target was in sight, but I wasn't utilizing any real mentorship. As a slow learner, it took me years before I could connect the dots. It was then that I went back to school to learn real estate development. I had already learned how to do engineer site design with the land subdivision parameters, drainage, topography, utilities, and traffic measures. I had just completed 956 units on the New Jersey waterfront, three commercial developments in New Jersey, and then was off to the New York City big leagues, the "all-star game," as one of my mentors Lou March, March Associates described it. "If you succeed in New York City, you can succeed anywhere in the world," he said, and he was right on!

And now there I was, going back to school to connect all the dots of engineering, building, and learning finance to become a true real estate developer. It might seem like starting a real estate development company is an overbearing or remarkable task; but the truth is that it is within reach so long as you put a thoughtful plan in place that is carefully executed. Here are the best next steps to get that done:

Get Educated. You do not need any special degree to set up your own real estate development company. However, I highly recommend that you either educate yourself or lean on mentors that have been there before. A mentor will help you save a ton of time, money, and massive headaches that could lead to a migraine. A mentor is worth their weight in gold because they will be by your side throughout your real estate development career to help you avoid pitfalls. I have several mentors in real estate and every area of life. Remember, it's about what you don't know, and acknowledging that fact allows the stars to align. This may lead you to recognize that you need to master new concepts and/or get a higher degree. So if you need them, for instance, you may decide to get a degree in engineering or construction finance; these can go a long way to help you excel in real estate development.

Build Strong Relationships. A successful real estate developer never underestimates the power of having strong relationships. Developers need to build their dream team and connections with lawyers, bankers, tenants, architects, engineers, and general contractors. They need to build these strong relationships with people in different professions to form a successful team that will bring together a successful project.

Cultivate Creativity. As noted at the outset, one of the personal development traits that helped me craft the Modern Wealth Building Formula was my creativity to envision what others can't see through the eyes of the developer. Real estate development requires creativity in negotiation, design development, building systems, and finish selections to maximize profits. Every real estate development project starts off with a schematic idea. This idea then transforms into a concept and the design development where focus is on detail, means, and methods building your development on paper. And it is creativity that develops the landscape and the many types of architecture, array of skyscrapers, green buildings, and renewable energy and environments where we currently work and live.

Build Risk Tolerance. There are many risks, and real estate development requires patience and perseverance to honor your word. Risk tolerance is an important part of real estate development and an important part of your success. It was a massive weight off my shoulder to realize that the challenges of real estate development and construction were the most important part of business. Running $300 million in construction is no easy task. It requires risk tolerance for sure if you want a life. And keep in mind you're accountable and the chief risk mitigator.

Develop Skills, Systems, and Talent. You will need a strong set of skills to succeed as a real estate developer. For instance, it is important to have excellent communication skills, good interpersonal skills, analytical skills, creativeness, and the ability to take initiative. In addition, be ready to put in longer working hours than you've done in the past.

Practice Until Permanent. A real estate development project takes time to complete and gives you plenty of time to practice with intent. It is crucial to focus on your personal improvement and increase your business acumen with commitment to Principal 20, Success Principals by Jack Canfield - *Continuous and Never-Ending Improvement.* That is why you shouldn't rush to avoid making costly mistakes. Remember, you must get Set, Ready, and then Shoot!

Find Capital. Like I said earlier, you can make a lot of money in development. The more capital you have in the beginning, the bigger slice of the pie you eat at the bargaining table. Starting a real estate development company is capital intensive and is very profitable and higher risk and yields a much higher reward. Not knowing the importance of the money and the funding lessons taught herein, I had to learn things the hard way. It's much better to be financially strong. No matter where you plan to raise funds—private investors, hard money and/or banks—you will still be asked and need to have somebody put up money for your skin to be in the game.

Of course, you are going to have a few bogies in your first few rounds of golf. But the key to all the major duties that a real estate developer must accomplish is to understand that problems are bound to happen. My motto is this: Let's focus 90 percent on the solution and 10 percent on the problem. A successful real estate developer should be able to deal with tight budgets, leaning buildings, housing authorities, and many other problems that will surely pop up along the way. It's all part of the game and a good day's work. Something my father always said was, "Give a man a good day's work. That's all they can ask, and they will always be grateful and return the benefit."

Starting Your Biz

Feeling confident? Ready to get started? My hope is that you are empowered and ready to begin. With a head full of steam, I want to walk you through the steps to start your own business and begin doing deals. It might feel overwhelming to consider the entire journey, but we will take this one step at a time to ensure that you are thoughtfully moving in the right direction.

Step 1: Get a Mentor

Why reinvent the wheel if you don't have to? Success leaves clues, and when you mirror and model mentors that have accomplished what you want to achieve, you will typically save an inordinate amount of time. Mentors have, in most cases, learned from the mistakes you must avoid, and if you want to spare yourself heartache and numerous unnecessary hours of learning, consider that a mentor offers you a shortcut on a silver platter. These are the only shortcuts I would suggest because they are guided from the firsthand experience of a pro.

Step 2: Choose Your Business Entity

This is where you will most likely feel some butterflies in your stomach if this is your first venture, an unusual cocktail mix of feelings from fear to exuberance. You might even ask yourself, "Can I do this?" Of course you can, or you wouldn't be reading this book.

What type of entity should you open? Depending on your long-term goals, you might choose one entity over another. When buying real estate, you should have each investment in a separate LLC to give you both tax advantages and the corporate shield for personal liability protection. However, you might want a layered structure with C-corp as an umbrella parent entity for numerous LLCs and subsidiaries owning each piece in your portfolio. It depends on long-term goals relative to the level of business and can be structured like this thereafter. Lean on your accountant and other business professionals to outline the pros and cons of each.

The purpose here is to form the company in the state's filing office of your choice to obtain your articles of organization generally filed at the Secretary of State's Office. Some will recommend an attorney to form an entity, but we form companies at incorporate.com followed by obtaining your EIN number online at irs.gov. Both of these steps will take no more than thirty minutes. Ultimately, to close the loop on your path to success with entity formation, you want to establish the operating ground rules in the LLC operating agreement.

Step 3: Select Your Company Name, Open a Bank Account, Set up a Website

Your next steps should include the thoughtful yet important actions of choosing a company name, opening a bank account, and setting up a website. Seems simple enough, right? But far too often I see real estate companies choose names that are impractical or make little sense. Pick something with some meaning to you that has some creative juice to it. You want something that will scream excellence and draw people in when they are investing in your company.

You can then take that name and open a bank account. I recommend that you open up separate bank accounts to keep your real estate entity funds separate from your personal funds. The operational structure protects the owner's assets and helps with bookkeeping. It can also help you track your business purchases.

And finally, set up a website. I cannot stress this enough. It is crucial to have a professional website that outlines your credentials, your mantra, and the type of services you offer. Even if you haven't closed one deal, don't hesitate to share with the world that you are here to stay and mean business.

Step 4: Create an Operating Agreement

Next, set up an operating agreement. This is especially important if you have partners. It is crucial to outline your relationship, responsibilities, and split of the money that will be coming in soon. A strong operating agreement should include the following:
- Ownership and Operations Rules
- Members' Percentage Interests
- Members' Rights and Responsibilities
- Voting
- Management Duties
- How Profits and Losses Are Handled

This might cost a little bit of money to initially set up, but you will be thankful to have it in place if there are any disagreements or issues between or amongst the owners.

Step 5: Establish Investors' Criteria

We touched upon investment criteria earlier and now emphasize it as the key to finding profitable real estate investments. Establishing criteria sets the stage for you to meet higher-level people, find better quality investments, and ultimately produce higher returns. The criteria allow you to sell yourself, your plan, and anticipation to positive result. It gives you confidence and a rule of thumb to move forward with knowing that syndication works. Knowing what the target looks like can help you find the right fit in your investors, but it can also help you avoid the ones that won't help you along the way.

Step 6: Fine-tune Your Presentation

Don't forget the old cliché, "Presentation is everything." Maintaining *a top-down thinking approach and annual investment in your personal performance training* will help lead you to create a presentation that truly sets you apart. A solid presentation will do a good job of outlining the opportunity, your credentials, investment structure, and opportunity for return. Each and every one of your potential investors likely has plenty of investment opportunities coming across his or her desk. You have to stand out and make a splash if you want to land the money.

Step 7: Find Partners and Establish Your Dream Team

Whether you prefer to be a lone ranger or love the idea of being lean and building with other people, it is important to carefully pick your partners and team. Especially when you want to take your investments to the next level, you will need partnerships to make it work. Building your winning dream team requires vetting, nurturing, and creating mutual benefits. Especially if you are taking on a project from the ground up, your dream team has to be capable of winning the gold medal for you. And you have to be a master of creating a mutual opportunity for your professional dream team. Having a dream team support your efforts is necessary, and your dream team will grow with you.

Step 8: Position Finances to Pursue Investments

Presentation again is important for financial positioning. In reality, you might only have one shot to pursue investors. It is crucial to be prepared with a strong approach to ensure you deliver investors a business plan, company deck, and presentation that will attract the attention you need to build and sustain a business. I highly recommend that you *become a precision listener and effective communicator both verbally and in writing.* Combining this approach with the communication skill set is a winner when raising money. Another factor for larger opportunities may require in-house underwriting capabilities for off-market deals to make it happen on a bigger scale. Ideal investments are typically off-market deals and will not have underwriting. And without it, you really don't have a verified feasibility and true exit strategy and you're left at a disadvantage with the numbers. This is where the rubber meets the road with the need for you to understand the numbers so you can underpromise, overdeliver, and confidently present an accurate bottom line. You can learn this process from studying financial analysis models on market deals and then create models for in-house use. And if this is not your bailiwick, there are real estate university students and college graduates that are wizards in financial modeling and analysis. My suggestion is to *learn the numbers needed for finance, not necessarily the math.*

Step 9: Effortlessly Find Properties

With everything in place, you can now work to find the right investment for you. Now remember, you just don't go buy your first site and develop it unless you are a little crazy like me. You must follow your plan and find a deal, verify if your investment is viable and profitable, perform a feasibility study, and acquire, finance, and facilitate it. Then, rinse and repeat. It is important to ensure that you don't get scorched on your first deal, reduce risk, and prevent the many pitfalls of real estate development that often occur. You can do this by starting small, learning the ropes with the more controlled deals, and only then ramping it up. For additional tips on finding commercial investments, please reference the website of my good friend and world renowned real estate investment authority Dolf de Roos, at dolfderoos.com.

Step 10: Master Property Control and Offer Techniques

The name of the game is to strike when the iron is hot and take the necessary steps to master how to gain property control with minimal money down. Gaining an ability to negotiate a nonrefundable deposit contingent upon due diligence and in some cases approval to change zoning and develop the property is ideal. So is taking advantage of what you've heard called land banks, property where an owner becomes a motivated seller after you educate them on how to turn their land into a bank by obtaining entitlement rights and developing the property to the highest and best use. This step is a true game-changer.

Step 11: Create Due Diligence Protocol

We've outlined the importance of due diligence as the context for just about every single deal. It will make or break you. It's a process that requires precision so that you are precise in your calculated risk. And there are many items to clarify and verify before you go hard on a deal. You don't want to lose your deposit on a clause where your money goes hard for some unforeseen reason because you don't have a due diligence protocol in place.

Step 12: Close the Deal

This is where you take your place at the driver's seat. The team underwriting the deal has ten other deals on their desk. Legal counsel has many clients besides you. Who's driving the ship? You have to stay on top of everything through delegation and hands-on attention—a daily gentle push to ensure that things are going as planned. I've found out too many times the hard way that I should have called a team member to determine if he or she was working on closing the deal. I was unaware or made an assumption that everything was just fine when we were, in fact, stagnant. If you are going to get in the business of real estate, you will find many different steps just to get to the finish line. You don't want to falter once you arrive. That is why it is crucial to close the deal once you find yourself close to the end zone.

Master these twelve steps and you will be off to the races. This is the real deal and the reason why I've not only started a real estate development company but also obtained tremendous fulfillment and passion along the way. I have a purpose bigger than myself and that's to help you make it happen. This is an invaluable type of preparation and level of mastery applied to real estate investing opportunities. There's a lot of blocking and tackling to get started and to succeed in this business, and my gridiron experience and 166 tackles my senior year in high school as an all-state linebacker has helped me along the way. There is a path for you to become a wildly successful real estate investor and business owner. But at the end of the day, it starts and ends with your passion to make this happen. And in the next chapter we will further explore just how you can turn your real estate investment business from your side hustle to your full-time gig.

If money is your hope for independence you will never have it. The only real security that a man will have in this world is a reserve of knowledge, experience, and ability.

Henry Ford, *industrialist and business magnate*

CHAPTER 8

QUIT! YOUR DAY JOB:
Turning Your Investments
into a Full-Time Business

At this point you should feel empowered to step into the wonderful world of real estate investing. You've taken thoughtful steps to set up your small business and begin talking to your colleagues about investing in it. But in this chapter, we will explore the idea of taking this to the next level and turning your small startup into a monumental success.

What if I asked you to take a one-question survey that included the straightforward question, "Do you love your job?" What would your answer be? I have found that most people say, "NO!" On the other hand, I actually loved my job, but I always knew there would be much more for me when I was unleashed and found my true potential. I knew I had to make a change to find my true calling and greatest life potential.

Funny enough, do you know that free coffee is one of the top five things employees want on the job in order to be happy? Crazy right? But nowadays, executives from around the world are hell-bent on employee engagement as one of their top five business strategies. That's because disengaged workers feel no real connection to their jobs and tend to do the bare minimum. Are you engaged in your work, optimistic, team-oriented, and consistently taking steps to go above and beyond? Or are you pessimistic, egocentric, and have a negative attitude in the office?

It may even be worse as you may be suffering from disengagement on the job. That's not what you want. It doesn't feel good every day to be incongruent with not having a sense of or following your true purpose. When faced with this dilemma myself, I realized how it might impact me not only at work but also in my personal life. This is supported by the results of the 2018 US Employee Engagement Trend study that found that 34 percent of all employees don't even like their jobs.

This statistic intrigued me and pushed me to consider why so many people were miserable in the workplace. This led me to an interesting answer, "Workism!" Derek Thompson wrote how "workism" is a new religion for many. "What is workism?" you might ask. It's the belief that work is not only necessary to economic production but also the centerpiece of one's identity and life's purpose, and the belief that any policy to promote human welfare must always encourage more work.

That belief seems to create a serious disconnect with such a high unfulfillment rate. When people's circumstances are not aligned with their plan, it messes with their identity because they connect circumstance with identity. This is not the case. Unfortunately, it can lead to a tailspin and dissatisfaction at work.

Inc.com posted a survey that reminded me why I wanted to leave my job. It was a widespread example of dissatisfaction, where 79 percent of respondents felt that they were not paid what they deserved (that was me), 56 percent said that skilled employees were not given recognition (that was me), and only 36 percent and 34 percent of respondents felt that they could rely on supervisor and colleague support. These numbers are staggering and lead us to one final inquiry: Why do people continue to suffer?

I'm not sure why people suffer and don't live their passion. The stats reminded me of the conversations during the magic moments with my girls, Alyse and Courtney. They each had their choice of exclusive magic moments with me that we would create together, that special time doing their favorite pastime that would never be forgotten. Alyse and I loved to go on special date nights at new restaurants where we would meet and compliment the chef. Courtney and I spent hours at various equine facilities as she grew to support her horseback training and equine competitions. And my message to both was to always follow your dreams and live your passion, and they did.

Alyse is doing graduate work in nutrition and Courtney is starting an MBA program in equine management. I did my best to remind them both to follow their passion and then figure out how to make money doing it. Don't spend time on a job that doesn't fulfill you or pay you what you are worth or that handcuffs you to the grind that may never end unless you choose to take action. It's not a decision. Decisions have reasoning. It's a choice. The choice: I choose to own my own real estate business because I choose to own my real estate business! That's it! You can make it happen!

Finding Purpose in Your Palace

What does it mean to find purpose in your place? Is it owning the Taj Mahal? Is it working to stop climate change? Maybe you're interested in just being a good person? The truth is that it doesn't matter what you chose to do so long as it is purposeful and meaningful to you. Real estate filled that void for me. And I believe it is one way you can literally have it all—financial freedom, opportunity, fulfillment. Sounds amazing, right? I know it does! But it might also seem extremely frightening to quit your job and take the plunge. Think about it for a second.

What would it look like to quit your job? That question has probably been stirring around in your subconscious as you think, *I'm not happy*. What would it be like to do what you want, when you want, and how you want? Is that possible? Or you may be asking yourself if you can earn your annual salary monthly. If you don't ask, you will not receive. If given the chance, the brain can answer any question within its reach. When thinking about whether you should quit your job, you might consider some additional questions like:

Does my dream job give me more flexibility?

Does it offer me more time off?

Can I work less and make more money?

These are just a few of the questions most of you might consider. But maybe more important than any of these is the following: What is your purpose? Don't worry if you cannot immediately find the answer. However, this is an important question to consider. While I have found that working for another person offers gratification, a feeling of safety, and consistency, working for yourself offers you the chance to deliver on your personal purpose, not someone else's.

You have more flexibility in your own business, you get to set your own schedule, and you can work less and make more money. That's the bottom line. And the beauty of this path is that every day has its own beauty and wonderful challenges. There has never been a day in my real estate and construction career where I've done the same thing twice. I have played all the roles, from inspector, then moved up the ladder to superintendent, to assistant project manager, project manager, senior project manager, project executive, VP, SVP, and now CEO. It has been a very meaningful path for me.

So what is this worth to you? Do fulfillment and happiness have a price tag? Or is it more of a sacrifice? How do you have it all, a successful business, relationships, and a cash cow of a portfolio to allow you to start truly living the dream? Like anything in life, you must give something to get something. It's a law of nature. So don't sacrifice your family life. The time with your children is a precious gift and for most of us, family is what we live for. There is an easier way that I want to share with you.

Creating Your Business

Once again, the basics to creating your business can be found in the previous chapter. As Grant Cardone quotes, "Success is your duty, obligation and responsibility" so I will spell it out from my experience. I must say it's a constant confidence builder and you will get knocked down eight times at minimum. You must constantly get up and just do it. Make your purpose bigger than yourself to allow you to not sweat the small stuff and have a tendency to focus on why you can't do it. It's a mind clustersuck that you need to wrestle with to get ready, aim, and shoot to hit your target goal.

You might ask, "Should I just quit my job and start?"

You should not quit your job before putting a thoughtful plan in place. A good friend of mine walked on fire with me at the Unleashed the Power event. Walking on fire makes you feel invincible. So he quit his job and he never really worked again with a purpose. Without a plan, he floundered for years. Now approaching sixty, he's broke and just got into real estate at the lowest level. It kills me to know that he had me as a mentor once and his blind spot was so big that he could not see how to have it all by NOT resisting suggestions. Don't do the same.

My approach was a little different. I worked day and night. I woke up at 5 a.m., as it was a MUST to be out the door before six or the traffic at Holland Tunnel would turn a thirty-minute drive into ninety minutes. Then I'd be on the job by 6:45 to hit shanties, where most men were preparing their tools before heading to the vertical ascend in the hoist to the upper floors for the start of the workday at seven. After a long half day that ended at dinner, I would attend master programs or study for my professional engineer's license till midnight. During the twenty years of this constant grind, I planned, spent hours analyzing the calculated risk, and feverishly learned and prepared for luck—preparation meeting opportunity!

How did I do that? Was it a side hustle and then a full-time job? It can be depending on what you decide to get into. If you are focused on getting started on residential, and I've seen many do the side hustle, you can do wholesale and fix and flips all day long while working within a system. You don't have to quit your job unless you choose to.

Transitioning into Great Opportunity

So what is the best transition from employee to employer? Are you ready to be your own boss? Do you understand what it takes to be accountable on you own? You don't have that daily routine that the workplace formulates for you, so you must have systems to hold you accountable and ensure you're on track to meet your goals and objectives.

As you are aware, my professional life didn't start as a business owner, nor did I even fathom the thought. Growing up in a blue-collar family, starting a business was not the main topic at the dinner table. The transition for me from salaried employee to entrepreneur was very rough, and it took a leap of faith to go from a salary of $175,000 to $60,000 per year in the beginning. I would have sworn to you I was ready, but I quickly learned that I wasn't nearly as ready for this ride as I had once thought. I really didn't have a total handle on what I was planning to do. My learning curve was very high, but it eventually leveled off.

Before just doing it, you should consider building up a savings fund, know the amount of income you need to quit, and know your potential to earn. The leap of faith should consider six months of living expenses. You should build up cash reserves and have a clear understanding of the monthly income you will need to cover your new lifestyle as an entrepreneur. Once you know how much money you need to quit, then you should have a full fee schedule so that you can fully understand your earning power and ability to scale your new business. Here are some of the most valuable lessons I learned when I started my own business:

You Will Work Weekends. If you think it's going to be easy to shut the lights off, you're mistaken. You will take your work home with you knowing you have to meet payroll and keep families fed. It's not just about the employees, and it's your job to go above and beyond. You will think about your company at night while home trying to relax, and you will most likely work weekends when getting started. Don't you recall hearing that your nine-to-five job pays the bills and any work thereafter is what builds your character and legacy?

Batten Down the Hatches. If you're not fortunate like me to have an ace in the hole (my dear wife who rocked the cosmetic bench with formulations and patents to allow us to have a safety net), then you better prepare for the worst. In those instances, you need to batten down the hatches. Sacrifice your expenditure in lieu of immediate gratification. The money will come, and you have to set parameters and discipline around the cash flow. It will make sense as you start to operate and cash flow goes out as fast as it comes in. And most importantly, if you have children, health insurance is a primary responsibility.

Set Yourself Apart. The good news is that this is your opportunity to shine. We've all heard the concept of a Unique Selling Point (USP). There is no competition when you set yourself apart, and this is why you want to create a niche market versus entering a saturated market where the piranhas are hanging out.

Establish Your Timeline. Perhaps the biggest adjustment from a traditional job to being self-employed is that there is no set schedule to follow. You MUST be disciplined as your own boss. Extended coffee breaks are permitted, however like anything else, you need to establish boundaries for yourself. Treat your business similar to your previous corporate job. Set a routine, stick to it, and give it your all. It's a privilege to be in business for yourself, and you don't want to fail.

Create a Transition Plan. Planning doesn't always sound that exciting, but putting together a transition plan is crucial for making sure that you're able to get everything done before you leave. It doesn't have to be fancy, especially if you're not the planning type, but I would recommend including at least this basic information:

- **Working Space.** One of the biggest changes to the business world is whether you need an office, especially when most people in real estate work remotely or in the field. To get started, you don't necessarily need an office. You can share offices or set up a home office where many businesses operate. In the past, if you wanted to make a good first impression, you needed to have a dedicated office space. However, with all the changes in technology, you can essentially work anywhere without an office or business card. All you need is a laptop, printer, and a table. Regardless of your choice, you ultimately need a mailing address and a space that works for you.

- **Archiving.** When most people leave their companies, they lose access to everything work related: email, documents, servers, professional development materials, and more. So make sure you set aside enough time to archive everything that's important to you. I created a Dropbox account and saved everything I thought might be needed for future access such as templates, reports, and other project data. Of course, you should not breach any confidential and disclosure issues.

- **Mentoring.** Always hire a mentor when opening a business. There are too many crossroads you can't afford to make a wrong turn on. Currently, I have nine coaches in many areas where growth is required. No one can afford to do things twice or prolong the learning period.

- **Networking.** There are a few reasons why networking is a critical part of your transition. The obvious reason is that networking can jumpstart your business and give you a chance to close deals quickly by what I refer to as creating membership amongst your peers. When you network, people learn about your new venture and the serving begins. The second reason may be more important. Networking gives you an opportunity to get out in your market and talk with other professionals. It can be a big adjustment going from working in an office where there could be dozens of people around you to sitting alone in your kitchen looking for deals. Networking allows you to hear other people's stories and in turn bounce your ideas off them. You never know—that one meeting you don't want to attend may be the one where you meet that one person who changes the game.

The truth is that there is nothing more frightening and exciting than starting your own business. There is just no feeling like it—the highs, the lows, the obstacles, and, of course, the wonderful success once you begin to hit your stride. Starting a business boils down to really mastering yourself and knowing your business like the back of your hand before going into your new venture with a blindfold on. You should know your area of expertise well enough to be able to write a book about it. Then, utilizing this high level of knowledge will help to offer you long-term sustainability and a remarkable ability to develop real estate and/or scale your existing business.

Whether we want to identify with it or not, what we do is almost as important as who we are. It impacts every last grain of your very existence. Thus, if you are content and happy then you will feel the same out of the office. But if you are discontent and lack purpose then you very well may struggle to not only be happy with your profession but also with your life as a whole. I started from nothing and have built my company into what I would humbly refer to as a success. But more crucial to my own life is that I feel purpose in my work. It is everywhere. I literally love what I do, which allows me to handle the long days and at times, sleepless nights. Armed with a purposeful endeavor, we can now turn our focus on some of the best tips to actually grow your business. In the next chapter, I will outline nine ways to earn fees in real estate development.

The successful warrior is the average man, with laser-like focus.

Bruce Lee, *actor and martial artist*

CHAPTER 9

FEE GOLD:

Leveraging Your Efforts and Team
to Create a Revenue Stream

As you likely know, the main objective of real estate investing is to invest money with a calculated risk to seek the highest rate of return. It's pretty simple and excites most people. But that wasn't good enough for me. I wanted more action. I simply needed more moving parts in real estate. Building skyscrapers didn't fully satisfy my attention. That's what led me to study this process in detail and find ten ways to earn fees, which is when things shifted into overdrive. I had not only figured out how to buy major real estate with no money down, but I had discovered the pot of fee gold at the end of the rainbow.

My next step was to execute the plan I outlined for you in the previous chapters. Luckily for me, it worked. I started to scale and couldn't do it all on my own. So I did what all great leaders do—I built a team and surrounded myself with some of the best in the business. Many of them were better than me in their respective areas of expertise, which helped us grow and evolve. There were many pieces to the real estate development puzzle, and my team was extremely qualified in helping me put this puzzle together. Remove even one piece and you couldn't finish the puzzle.

Now that you are getting serious about real estate investing and working to create a company or business, not just a hobby, it is important to build your team. You've heard me mention the term "dream team," a nickname for the 1992 Olympics United States Men's Basketball Team that was literally stacked with talent. This is the type of team I formed on my first real estate development project. I kind of realized the enormous value by accident right after we secured approval to break ground on a huge development. We had essentially won the gold that night at the planning board meeting after fifty people stood and objected to our plan. We were within code, our plan made sense, and we had the township behind us because of the team we had sent to play the game overcame all objections.

In basketball, you have five players on the court that comprise your starting lineup. These key players need to stay healthy to maintain high odds for that team to make the playoffs. That team has depth on the bench to support the starting lineup to bring the team to the level where they may win the NBA championship or the Gold Medal in our Olympics analogy. These players on the court include a center, two forwards and two guards, and seven substitutes or bench players.

Real estate is the same way. So now it's appropriate at this time to take a deep look at the team required to perform real estate development. These include architects and engineers and contractors playing at various levels to serve the demands of specific investments.

Why is it so important to have a winning team? One reason is that you might want to complete projects on time and within budget. The other reason is to make some money. So how do you approach making money with control and cost savings? You as the developer are the king of the hill and are responsible for ensuring that everyone on your team is fully engaged and ready to go. Players may wait on the bench for many months at a time and then have to step in according to the schedule and hit a grand slam. Your real estate dream team should consist of some combination of the following:

Architects. These are the leaders of the design team and the people who plan, design, and review the construction of your buildings. Architects play an integral part in the project, as they should be full time and on call until the last person moves in the doors to satisfy punch lists and issues related to multiunit developments. They also provide services in connection with the design of the buildings and the space within the site surrounding the buildings that have human occupancy or use as their principal purpose.

Construction Manager or General Contractor. These positions oversee and lead a range of building projects from beginning to end. They are responsible for setting and keeping schedules, monitoring finances, and making certain that everybody is doing what they should. Construction managers and GCs are usually on site and dealing with the day-to-day activities and moving pieces.

Civil Engineers. These guys create, improve, and protect the environment in which we live. They plan, design, and oversee construction and maintenance of building structures and infrastructure, like roads, railways, airports, bridges, harbors, dams, irrigation projects, power plants, and water and sewerage systems. You will likely need to interact with civil engineers to deal with the relationship between your project and the environment around it.

Professional Planners. They help create a broad vision for the community. They also research, design, and develop programs, lead public processes, effect social change, perform technical analyses, manage, and educate the surrounding citizens about the projects and their potential impact on the community.

Zoning Consultant. These folks offer comprehensive planning, revitalization, and zoning services to a wide range of communities— large and small, urban and rural, cities and townships—and development services to the private sector. They ensure that your projects are properly zoned so you can secure permits and other government licensing in order to move forward and build.

Transportation Consultant. He or she is a specialist form of civil engineer whose purpose, through a variety of detailed studies and modeling techniques, is to provide the efficient movement of people and goods in the safest and most sustainable manner possible. Transportation (or lack thereof) has a great impact on any project, big or small.

Environmental Consultant. They should have deep knowledge of environmental regulations, which they can advise particular clients in the private industry or public government institutions about, to help them steer clear of possible fines, legal action, or misguided transactions. Environmental consulting spans a wide spectrum of industry.

Land Use and Zoning Attorneys. These lawyers' job is to advise regarding real estate development. This will include zoning laws and building ordinances as well as construction permits and other land use ordinances. They will work closely with real estate agencies, courts of law, title companies, and other agencies as required to ensure that you are not violating any local or state laws as you develop your project.

Real Estate Attorney. He or she is often equipped to prepare and review documents related to real estate. This includes items like purchase agreements, mortgage documents, title documents, and transfer documents. In most cases, the real estate attorney provides legal guidance for individuals relating to the purchase or sale of real property.

Expeditor. This is someone who facilitates a process, whether it be something as simple as securing a permit or something much greater as getting the schematics or blueprints approved by the city. It is a position or role found within project management, construction, purchasing, production control, and New York City permitting.

Surveyors. Surveyors update boundary lines and prepare sites for construction so that legal disputes are prevented. Surveyors make precise measurements to determine property boundaries, elevations of floors, plumpness of columns, and interior layout. They provide data relevant to the shape and contour of the Earth's surface for engineering, mapmaking, and construction projects.

Cost Estimators. They collect and analyze data to estimate the time, money, materials, and labor required to construct a building, develop the land, or provide a service. They generally specialize in areas of expertise and support financial feasibility analyses in real estate investing.

Geotechnical Engineers. This is one of my civil engineering specialties that uses principles of soil mechanics and rock mechanics to investigate subsurface conditions and materials, determine the relevant physical/mechanical and chemical properties of these materials, evaluate stability of natural slopes and manmade soil deposits, and assess the risks posed by site conditions.

Mechanical, Electrical, and Plumbing (MEP) Engineer. This is a single-level professional classification responsible for planning and design in the areas of mechanical, electrical, and plumbing (MEP) systems including design documentation, specifications, and inspection and commissioning procedures.

Marketing Consultant. Marketing plays an important role in establishing relationships between customers and an organization's offering to the market. The marketing consultant is also tasked with branding of the organization, participation in publicity activities, advertising, and customer interaction through feedback collection.

Investment Banker. Investment banks play a key role in helping companies and government entities obtain capital financing. As financial advisors to their clients, they help to price capital, allocate resources, and manage investments.

Mortgage Broker. A mortgage broker acts as a middleman between you and potential lenders. The broker's job is to work on your behalf with several banks to find mortgage lenders with competitive interest rates that best fit your needs.

Project Accountant. This position holds off auditors and works to ensure that companies or organizations are efficiently operating. They do this by accessing financial records of their clients. Duties include analyzing data, finance reports, budgets, tax returns, and accounting records.

Asset Manager. Simply put, asset management firms manage funds for individuals and companies. They make well-timed investment decisions on behalf of their clients to grow their finances and portfolio. Working with a group of several investors, asset management firms can diversify their clients' portfolios.

Real Estate Broker. A real estate broker is an individual or firm that charges a fee or commission for executing buy and sell orders submitted by an investor. A broker also refers to the role of a firm when it acts as an agent for a customer and charges the customer a commission for its services.

Lighting Consultant. Lighting designers in the arts create the light plot or outline for a show. They create a lighting design that will properly showcase the performers and the setting, varying the design throughout the production to meet the action on stage. Lighting designers typically do not manage the lights during the show.

Controlled Inspectors. In addition to third party inspectors, the 1968 Building Code allows for professional engineers and licensed architects to conduct required inspections during the construction process. These inspections were initially called Controlled Inspections, now referred to as Special Inspections, and ensure that work is safe and being constructed according to approved plans and specifications.

Exterior Wall Consultant. He or she specializes in design, investigation, repair, and management of roofing, exterior wall, and waterproofing systems. During the construction phase, the facade consultant oversees the installation of envelope systems, including windows and doors, to ensure that they are faithfully following design and code requirements. In the long run, investing in a building consultant can save you a lot of money.

Elevator Consultant. An elevator consultant is someone who specializes in the design, testing, and maintenance inspection of elevators, escalators, moving walkways, and many other conveyances that move people. They are not to be confused with elevator mechanics. Consultants (unlike mechanics) do not normally perform work on conveyances.

As you can see, there are likely dozens of different team members that might chip in and provide insight into building a skyscraper. You would likely need far less of these team members if you were to flip a house, build new construction, or even create a multiunit dwelling. However, it is crucial to understand the widespread scope of people available to you and your team. Don't cut corners or feel that your architect can handle your zoning or variances. You couldn't be more mistaken, and you will likely spend much more money on the backend fixing the issues that a nonqualified professional might cause for you.

Carefully survey each of these potential positions and consider what you need before the ink even dries on the contract.

Leveraging Your Efforts

Now that you have your plan to move forward and a thoughtful and strategically created team in place to execute it, start thinking about how you are going to leverage your efforts. You might ask some important questions at this juncture: "What is it that I need to do to succeed in the real estate business? What is my marketing approach? How can I tap into network groups? Where are weekly project meetings? Who do I pitch?" Now that you've gained an understanding of the approach, you have to dig in and prepare yourself to execute it. To that end, it would be helpful to envision a day in the life of running and managing the activities of a real estate development and investment company.

The best part of this is that almost every day is totally different. You are rarely solving the same problem or wearing the same hat. Real estate has a plethora of disciplines and professions and the opportunity to learn about them all with the peace of knowing you have a team member that has your back.

The way I leveraged my efforts was to always be thinking using the Critical Path Method (CPM), a concept developed by the US Navy and used in building the World Trade Center in 1966. We learned this in engineering school, focusing on scheduling, critical paths, predecessors, successors, and how all these concepts apply to life. This way of thinking allows me to determine which tasks are "critical" (i.e., on the longest path) in any project or undertaking and which have "total float" (i.e., can be delayed without making the project longer). If you think about it, whether you are running your family or building skyscrapers, the critical path is the sequence of activities that add up to the longest overall duration of what you are trying to accomplish, regardless of float. This determines the shortest time possible to complete the project. So how does this apply to your real estate business?

Thinking like this can help to reduce the cost of your most expensive commodity—time. There are only so many hours in the day, and it is important that you work with a critical path mode to meet your deadlines. Thus, leverage your efforts with mentors, systems, and technology to Eliminate, Delegate, and Automate (EDA). Eliminate everything you should not be doing, delegate everything possible, and automate till the sun doesn't shine. Think about the possibilities for a positive impact on your business and life with CPM and EDA thinking. The sky's the limit.

With any business investment or development plan, I highly recommend thinking through each task or activity to meet your short- and long-term goals. Once you outline your activities, you can then determine duration and relationship to the predecessors and successors for each activity to develop how the activities interrelate to one another. This CPM schedule exercise is a must for me because it helps me clearly understand the sequence of events as well as targeting milestones, scheduled completion dates, and my overall goals.

As you complete this process, the momentum starts to move rapidly. Thus, it is important that you develop your team and align them to your long-term strategies with mutual benefit.

With all the activities going on in any one given day as a developer, it's hard to turn the lights off. However, the fee gold at the end of the rainbow and potential revenue as a developer is something to write home to Mom about.

The Revenue Streams

At the end of the day, the goal of building a strong team is to create a successful business that generates revenue and, ideally, multiple income streams. One night, as I stepped outside for my daily walk and worry about money and supporting my family, I sat down on my patio and gazed up at the stars. I was worrying night after night on my walk and finally blurted at the stars, "Twins, how am I going to do this ?" Oddly enough, while looking up at the stars there was a connection of each star to a player on the development team. In that moment, I realized that I had many of the skills in areas of the development process where we could bring value to the investment.

I sat in awe for a minute as I ran numbers in my head on a $10 million development. Could it be true as the numbers reflected huge opportunity? With many areas of expertise in mind, the fees that could be pulled in-house if my team could only provide an equal or greater service for less money were substantial and a game-changer. These were fees that had to be paid out, in any event, to others, and with our trusted relationship we felt confident that our investors would see that it made sense to pay us.

When you see the various fees discussed herein, you can see how I was able to generate substantial fees of more than 20 percent of total cost. That's over $2 million in potential fees alone for being hands-on and vertically integrated in-house with skill sets, and if the day-to-day meets your lifestyle like it did for me, I went full time. Could this be double dipping? No, it's legitimate. You disclose and are proud of it because you are delivering in accordance to your promises and have provided the investment with less expense and higher returns. That's what investors are looking for, and they should not be looking at your pocket if they are sophisticated investors and see the advantage of vertically integrated firms. Could this be the sunrise I was looking for or the fee gold at the end of the rainbow?

As I pondered this thought, I also wondered how I could generate fee gold at the beginning of the rainbow to enable us to run the business if the strategy worked. I would have to figure out how to structure the deal where I could contract with myself to be the developer, which I was not sure how to do at first. So off to my advisors I went.

I could not sleep for the next few nights, knowing it was possible to start a business on a shoestring budget by myself. But I realized with a development fee of 5 percent of the total project cost, I could earn more than $600,000 (excluding any construction management or other fees) on one deal. That was an eye-opener.

So I started to pay myself fees to provide a service to the investment group with which I was working. Since they were going to pay the fee either way, it made sense to give me a shot. In doing so I saved them money, did a better job because of my personal interest, and was able to start my own business. I'm not saying developers are looking for the pot of fee gold, as they are primarily focused on personal investment, investor relations, and positive returns. It was different in my case as I didn't have much money, so we had to stay afloat. This forced a strategy of a fee developer actually working my business for the fees as developer and construction manager initially where I could hang on to a small piece of ownership for facilitating the deal because of the lack of personal equity.

Thus, there is great value in looking at the potential profits and fees that can be generated by an investor/developer/builder who is vertically integrated with in-house services and a strong team. As you can see from the players on the dream team, various services you could pay for might be conducted in-house instead. Here are some:

Acquisition Fee. Acquisition fees may be referred to as charges and commissions that one pays for the lease, acquisition, or purchase of property, such as closing costs, real estate commission, and development and/or construction fees. From observations and experience, this is also referred to in some instances as what I call connector fees earned when bringing parties together to consummate a transaction. This fee is also negotiable and can range from 1 to 10 percent.

Pros: This is great for starters to target and establish themselves as players on larger scale deals. This is a form of bird-dogging where you bring buyers and sellers together and charge a fee.

Cons: When you snooze, you lose. Have an agreement that you carry in hand to lock up your piece of the pie before you start connecting with people. How many times have you teed up a deal and suddenly lost your piece of the pie?

Finance Fee. The finance charge is any fee representing the cost of credit or the cost of borrowing. It can be a combination of a transaction fee, interest accrued on and fees charged for some forms of credit increase or a loan for a period. It includes not only interest but other charges as well, such as financial transaction fees. In some states, usury laws allow charges as high as 18 percent and if you're bringing money to the table you are entitled to compensation. In an ideal circumstance, you can carve a point for yourself.

Pros: Funding real estate transactions is an active market where many opportunities exist to further capitalize when you're positioned for the acquisition fees of bringing people together. Once together, you bring another solution to the table for a fee.

Cons: Complex capital stacks may create legalities and require workarounds in the instance of raising money under securities regulations.

Marketing Fee. This is a relatively large fee in major developments that includes branding, building models, television, radio, books, and brochures. You may be able to provide portions of the marketing strategy, however you don't want to be pennywise and dollar foolish as this will make or break a project. To target this fee internally, you must be equipped to deliver the best marketing material in the interest of the investment or otherwise hire the best firm necessary to sell your project at the highest sale price on the market.

Pros: This practice can lead to a large fee if equipped to capture these opportunities by providing your client with the marketing materials.

Cons: This may distract your development team from their primary focus of development and sales strategies. It might make sense to leave this to the experts.

Sales Fee. This is a fee charged by a broker or agent for his/her service in facilitating a transaction, such as the buying or selling of securities or real estate. In the case of securities trading, brokers can be split into two broad categories depending on the sales fees they charge.

Pros: Your ability to leverage this fee will either reduce the total fee on sales or enable you to share. Brokers are hungry and will work with you when they see you are savvy to the deal.

Cons: The depth of your sales force will now be available if you do this internally versus having to outsource this to a Corcoran or a Douglas Elliman.

Owner's Representative Fee. This is someone who acts as a representative for the owner of a real estate development or a construction project and charges fees on the day-to-day responsibilities associated with this job. Do not confuse an owner's representative with a project manager though, as the owner's rep handles all aspects of the development versus a project manager, who manages certain processes and is one of many project people. Fees can come in the form of a lump month sum, a fee based on percentage of budget, or an monthly range of $15,000 to $30,000 per month.

> **Pros:** This is an easy step in the evolution to charge on your own investments and development.

> **Cons:** You lose if you choose not to learn how to manage the process and get paid for it.

Development Fee. A developer's fee is compensation for the developer's time and for taking on the risk of developing a commercial or residential construction project. The fee is a percentage of the total cost of development, in the range of 3 to 8 percent.

> **Pros:** This is a substantial fee used to pay for staff and overhead.

> **Cons:** You cannot capture this fee unless you've been around the block a few times or if you partner with a fee developer and they share the fee with you or pay for your monthly obligation.

Construction Fee. A fee for acting as general contractor (GC) and/or construction manager (CM) to construct improvements, supervise and coordinate projects, or provide major repairs or rehabilitations on a property. A typical general conditions and fee profit ranges 10 to 20 percent and would translate, on a job budgeted at $20 million, to funds flowing into your company in the range of $1 million to $2 million for the manager's services. Another advantage of your ability to act as general contractor or construction manager is that you will retain a high degree of control and involvement in the process.

> **Pros:** You will have control and a respectable profit margin.

> **Cons:** There is more risk, and it requires experience not to crack your teeth on this attempt.

Options and Upgrades Fees. Average Cost of Upgrades, Price Range and Upgrades.

The average cost of new home upgrades per house is about 10 percent of the cost of the home, but that average does not hold consistent throughout the market. Homes with a base price of $180,000 or less averaged upgrades of about 7.3 percent. I've sold finish upgrades and have earned an additional 3 to 5 percent in profit.

Pros: This is money you will otherwise leave on the table.

Cons: A sales model and capital expenditure are required at the outset of sales.

Asset Management Fee. A management fee is a periodic payment that is paid by an investment fund to the fund's investment advisor for investment and portfolio management services. Usually, the fee of 1 percent is calculated as a percentage of assets under management.

Pros: This is a shoe-in if you are in the business and you want to manage your own assets, therefore taking advantage of this overhead reimbursement.

Cons: It requires precision and attention to ensure stabilization and accuracy.

Property Management Fee. Typical fee agreement as a baseline, expect to pay a typical residential property management firm where fees range between 5 to 8 percent of the monthly rental value of the property, plus expenses. Some companies may charge, say, a $100 per month flat rate.

Pros: If you are set up managing your own properties and have staff to support growth, it's the next step in the evolution to keep you in the game with your bread and butter.

Cons: Your company will receive calls in the middle of the night with dirty jobs and headaches.

If you want to secure pure fee gold then you have no choice but to leverage your efforts and team to create a revenue stream. Money may not be the predominant reason why you chose to build your own real estate business, but it is a wonderful ancillary effect of doing great work. But in the end you are only as strong as the quality of your team. Whether you choose to outsource or hire permanent positions so you can handle clients' needs in a turnkey manner, it is vital to thoughtfully structure your team to meet your internal needs and the external desires of your clients. Do that and you are destined for fee gold.

"Let no feeling of discouragement prey upon you, and in the end you are sure to succeed."

Abraham Lincoln, *former president of the United States*

CHAPTER 10

DON'T STEP IN IT!
The Twelve Unmistakable Myths
of Commercial Real Estate

I t doesn't matter what industry or profession you are in . . . myths happen. You know, those seemingly true and widely accepted concepts that are really just misleading dirty rumors that can impact your perspective on how to run your business? When gathering my thoughts on the myths we often see in real estate, all I could think about were the witches in Salem, a traditional story concerning the early history of people and social phenomena. Therefore, I never really considered the impact of myths on my real estate journey until I actually thought about them. Sure enough, many came to mind about the false beliefs that initially stopped me from taking the next step in real estate. My hope is that in this chapter you will learn from some of the biggest mistakes and beliefs I had early on.

Over the past thirty years, I've learned a lot about real estate investing and development. As you know from my stories, I learned the hard way through costly experiences, spending an inordinate amount of time on education. Even then, I still made several mistakes along the way. When I decided to start my own business, I made a list of all the potential mistakes I might make, with the hope of avoiding them.

There were more than 100 items on that first list, and I kept adding to it. After learning how to dodge many of these bullets, I turned it into a special report to share with fellow investors and people wanting to learn about or expand in real estate investing. The report is called the "11 Secrets of Real Estate Investing and the 60 Pitfalls to Avoid" and you can obtain This chapter boils this initial report down to the most valuable lessons for you relative to your limiting beliefs. I also recommend that you read Jack Canfields' Success Principals, Principle 33, "Transcend Your Limiting Beliefs."

I've learned that many misconceptions circulate about real estate. My goal in this chapter is to help dispel these myths so that you can save yourself from inaction, analysis paralysis, and indecisiveness. In addition, I've added a personal strategy that I used to overcome these false beliefs.

These myths are relative to all real estate transactions, and my hope is that you receive them in context relative to your own situation and goals. The insights that follow are intended to identify and dispel the myths and misconceptions experienced in commercial real estate with firsthand facts and to offer my strategy that will enable you to level the playing field in your beliefs about commercial real estate investing and development.

Fifteen Unmistakable Myths

Myth #1: You need money or good credit to get started.

Facts: You don't need any money to get started in commercial real estate. I had a job, six-figure debt, and a low credit score. Not only do banks care more about the potential profit of the property than your actual bank account, you most likely will not have a deep enough pocket without a personal guarantor anyway. So don't start sweating it already.

You can consider my path as an option with syndication at any level of real estate. Understand that there are also private moneylenders that are willing to lend you what you need if the numbers on commercial deals are promising.

I also see the nature of commercial real estate shifting with forth-coming currency and technology advancements, where at some point nearly all investors will choose to leverage profits by *borrowing the money* to finance a new investment. This will enable more investors to enter the commercial real estate structures you create.

Now, if you just want to park a little cash, there are opportunities to invest as little as $5,000 to $10,000 with wholesalers always looking to mitigate for cash-flow limitations. Thus, you don't have to be rich to get started.

Strategy: Consider the truth of these facts relative to your personal bank account and credit score. If you're still freaked out, consider a partnership where your partner is better suited with possible banking relationships. This will give you the confidence to approach underwriting early in the process to confirm their focus on the entity and the property's anticipated performance.

Myth #2: You must already be rich and have lots of money to get financing.

Facts: You don't have to be rich to do this. If you have your feet on the ground and you're coachable, you can make nice money in commercial real estate deals if you choose a syndication route and lack finance capabilities. However, you will need to step up big time as the maestro, the connector of a group of investors and facilitator of the investment process bringing opportunity to investors. In return, you get your piece of the action in the deal. In doing so, you can also retain certain controls without your own money if you know what you're doing as someone responsible for day-to-day decision-making.

When I purchased my first major deal, a twelve-acre site for a $25,000 refundable deposit, I was even deeper into my financial situation just described after buying 300 diapers and 1,440 ounces of formula for twelve consecutive months. Breastfeeding could not keep up with demand of two babies both born at almost eight pounds. We owned a modest house when interest rates were 18 percent. We had a load of bills and credit card debt. Even though it was a different world, this situation applies for many today who have successfully obtained financing on their commercial deals.

That's why this is the biggest myth of all—that commercial investing requires a large bankroll to finance. While it's true that commercial properties have more zeros and therefore require larger capital investment as noted in an earlier chapter, I can personally confirm that this myth is just not true.

Strategy: Consider this all a mindset and a mental battle with yourself to choose that you are enough to make it happen regardless of where you are financially. You have to look past the "what's so"—your current circumstance—and seek a new blueprint on life with light at the end of the tunnel. You can do this! I've proven it at every level and was stopped dead in my tracks many times as our natural mindset is to look at the negative.

Myth #3: You must spend time on small deals before you can do a big deal.

Facts: Other than buying my house, my first deal was $17 million. It was a big deal for sure, and you don't need to put your time in on small residential deals to be able to get into commercial deals. I went for the gusto the first time because I realized that construction of a 100-unit vertical skyscraper was essentially the same as a ninety-unit horizontal assisted living facility, rinse and repeat. This skill set would apply to any construction project, and it was more myself that would hold me back if I did sting when the iron was hot. The frontend and backend were essentially the same except the skyscraper duration for those activities was much longer so it was all relative.

Now, I'm not saying you will have this much confidence with what you know. However, your experience can apply by bridging the gap or depending on an owner's rep and your construction manager to get it done. All you have to do is get the right team and they make you succeed, because it's now bigger than, and no longer only about, you.

Strategy: Be openminded from the outset to find a large profitable deal that works and believe that people want to help you accomplish your outcomes. Remember, I had no idea how to develop a 113-bed assisted living facility. I just kept asking the right question to surround myself with the right team and then managed to direct people accordingly and make it to the goal line. You can do exactly what I did when you put your mind to it.

Myth #4: You must have a lot of free time to make more money.

Facts: You do not need a lot of free time to invest in commercial real estate. If you want to take on a major real estate development described herein, you may be forced to choose a new career path with cash flow persuasion. To be clear, it is not a full-time job unless you choose to take on the construction. If you are not a contractor or have built for others, you will enjoy being a developer having this responsibility on someone else's shoulders.

If you apply the techniques of fee gold and the Modern Wealth Building Formula in your approach, you'll learn how to keep your time invested in a commercial project to ten to twenty hours a week or less. While you can dedicate a lot of time to invest in real estate, it's not a requirement. I know commercial investors who work twelve-hour days, own twenty-plus units and office buildings, and still have time to travel the world and enjoy life.

Investing in real estate does not have to take a lot of time. What can take time is building your investment or development team, and then once you've assembled that team it requires less time and effort. As we hammered home in the last chapter, choosing the right team members is the key to building your business and minimizing your time requirement.

Again, time management consideration is your preference on role, passive or active, and another instance where the type of investment property you choose to invest in makes a big difference along with the lifestyle you have. Many types of commercial income properties are totally passive, while others—particularly development or major add-value renovations to increase equity—are concentrated, labor intensive, and require the necessary expertise to complete the project expeditiously.

Looking at the bright side, after your first deal, you will have learned the ropes and your allocated time will be more effective on new deals than on working in your day job, which is the goal we are striving for. With all this said, understand that increasing deal size is not directly proportional to absorbing more of your time. Especially when systems are in place to ensure an investment property is running smoothly, which is a MUST to prevent unnecessary time absorption from your personal life..

Strategy: Obtain more time management tools and systems, establish improvement in your effectiveness goals quarterly, take copious notes on all that you learn, and continuously seek knowledge or mentorship to elevate yourself to the next level.

Myth #5: You must be an experienced investor.

Facts: I had construction experience, book knowledge, and was $60,000 in the hole. There had to be a better way, however I did not have any real estate investing experience and had to sink or swim. We all have to start somewhere, and this is where I took on the approach of my top-down thinking on a project outside the Big Apple, and it was a home run.

I learned by cracking my teeth, let's say the hard way, like the people I've seen. People go through massive sacrifice and trial and error only to come up short. They pay the price the whole way, whereas you don't have to pay such a price if you're open to my strategies.

There is no way any one person can know everything. The most important thing you need to know is what goal you are looking to achieve and then what strategies you will use and where to source investment opportunities that will help you achieve that goal. I've spent countless hours documenting all the different investment strategies and compiling all the most important information that a person would need to know to master or get started investing. The information is out there and as a friendly reminder, the resources are available. It's the accountability of your resourcefulness that counts!

Strategy: Surround yourself with experienced team players to overshadow you if necessary, utilize associates in the business on your deck to improve credibility, and follow the bridge that closes the gap that you build to cross. Consider that this process of building your credibility and presentation is like a recipe—you must obtain ingredients for it, read instructions, and proceed with preparing and cooking the meal. The same analogy goes for a lack of experience in real estate. Just do it!

Myth #6: Good commercial deals are hard to find.

I'm curious, what is your meaning of a good deal? If you recall the section in an earlier chapter on investor criteria, this is what I consider the parameters of a good deal for you and your partners: Deals suit all types of individuals in different ways, and the term "good" is individualized and subjective. As Dolf de Roos details in his book *Commercial Real Estate Investing*, there are many ways of finding great commercial real estate deals.

The bottom line is that there are always good investment opportunities available in commercial real estate.

Strategy: Believe you can find great deals, clearly understand the parameters of a good deal, envision yourself finding a great deal, create a collage of the great commercial deals that you want to find, hang the collage on your wall, and look at in the morning and at night before you go to bed. Leverage this belief with your dream team to find the great deal that meets your investment criteria, and you will find a great deal.

Myth #7: You must face a complicated transaction because the numbers are harder.

Facts: This is not math. Learn what the numbers mean. It's not hard, and I know that if I can figure out calculus II after failing twice, you can figure out how to understand the numbers to make money in real estate. Think of immigrants that come to our country and figure it out. Why can't Americans do it?

While you definitely want to make sure the numbers pencil out on any deal, don't assume you'll be sitting at that desk with a calculator. That's the exact reason why I left engineering. I could not sit still.

Usually, you'll just need to make sure you have the financial information needed to analyze the deal, and then that information will be plugged into the software or in-house model to give you all the details necessary to make a decision. Having these in-house capabilities are beneficial. They can also be supported through third-party assistance and essential to expeditiously performing a financial feasibility analysis to obtain off-market deals.

Strategy: Think simple. Price, cash to close, annual return on cash and long-term yield. Getting to those numbers is not difficult, however if you don't do it every day, you can find formulas online and there are many people available that help with a quick paper napkin or full-blown financial analysis. In these cases, where only raw data is available, you hire someone to help you with the numbers. This allows you to stand behind your creativity to find more and learn how to make a deal work.

Myth #8: If I don't manage residential then commercial is out of my league for sure.

Facts: Commercial real estate and residential real estate are two different animals altogether.

While you can choose to double your time on your real estate investments by being overactive or becoming the property manager, it makes more sense both financially and timewise to hire a management service for commercial real estate.

The profits you make in commercial real estate are higher than in residential real estate, thus making it financially viable to hire a management company. Property management companies manage several properties and typically have critical mass, economies of scale, and dollar-cost averaging for repairs and other means to manage your property cheaper than you can as an individual investor.

Strategy: Unless you are close in proximity, equipped with systems and a critical mass of staff managing other properties, hand over this responsibility to an experienced property manager while you make sure all your deals can afford one.

Myth #9: The majority of commercial income properties are advertised.

Facts: Similar to the job hunt, there is only a fraction of the jobs (properties) advertised and shown online relative to the number of actual jobs (properties) available. The approach of bandit signs won't work for commercial properties. It's a presentation ball game indicating you are ready for this league. Why? Because of those thousands of properties advertised, only a few mention prices. You need to know how to, or have someone who can, talk turkey with the ability to have someone run some numbers so you can make a move. On the other hand, those properties that do mention prices are typically stripped of any substantial profits, and comparables are limited.

Strategy: This is where ML and AI strategies come into play and tasking local experts for data that's not privy. These experts are in the trenches and in most cases can obtain relatively accurate information even if you can't visually see a lease or operating agreement. When you gather a variety of information from various local experts, you can triangulate information into data that will enable you to act onto the next step. As you learn markets that offer profitable deals, I'm sure you will quickly establish your own database.

Myth #10: You must take risks or, worse, big risks.

Facts: You won't take any more risk than you would take on any other real estate investment.

Risk must be calculated no matter how many zeros, and there is no finite formula for risk. The financial risk is essentially on the investor; however, your reputation is on the line and always at risk no matter the size of your deal.

Commercial real estate investments are like any other investments; your level of risk depends on what you choose to invest in personally. Every business venture involves risk, and commercial real estate investment is no exception. The question is, "What is the degree of risk?" Can we calculate and mitigate risk, and does that risk outweigh the potential reward?

Let's say a residential property costs you $100,000, while a commercial property costs you $500,000. Does the commercial property represent a 500 percent higher risk? If you know what you're doing, probably not.

Strategy: Your mindset must believe in calculated risk that prevents losses and that this is the "what's so" of real estate. That's what stockbrokers do. Make sure their stock trade wins are more than their stock trade losses. If you have a stable investment, there is always a risk of a tenant going out of business or moving out; and it's calculated that based on the grade of your investment, it will attract another tenant. Plan your exit strategies and mitigation steps like an emergency recovery plan for a major corporation.

Myth #11: You must either be part of the elite, born into an ultrarich family, or have "connections" in city hall or high places.

Facts: You don't need to be part of the elite class, an ultrarich family, or be "connected" to do commercial deals. If there is not a seat at the table, you make one. I grew up in a middle-class family and went from a ten-dollar per week stipend in college to a millionaire without being part of an elite or ultrarich group, nor did I know anyone in Bridgewater, New Jersey, when I purchased the property.

Strategy: Take the steps recommended in this book to attract the elite ultrarich and get connected so your six degrees of separation can get you to anyone on the planet.

Myth #12: You must be a white guy in an Armani suit who lives in the city.

Facts: All brothers and sisters WANTED!

You don't have to be some big wig. You don't have to be male. And you don't need to be white.

This formula works for anyone. Your race, creed, or color has no bearing on your success. You can be, act, and dress like yourself and still succeed in commercial real estate.

Strategy: You must understand this fact and strategy. Enter an industry that has produced more millionaires than any other and DOES NOT require a formal education because you essentially have free entry into real estate, and I'm here to say that there are NO EXCUSES for you not to jump in head first.

Myth #13: You must be older, or I'm too old to start something that big.

Facts: Your age has no bearing on real estate investing or development.

I wish to have started when I read *No Money Down* at eighteen. Oh well. It's never too late, regardless of age. I've heard of a child buying real estate at age eleven. Now, if you follow Dan Sullivan's theory, he believes that he will live to 120 years old, which gives a whole new perspective on life if you think about it for a few minutes. My first thought was, *WOW, I can extend my internal deadline. LOL.* There are so many advantages in real estate for any age group. If you are young, you have a lifetime journey, and if you are older you have to get busy now. Whatever your age, you are living a new passion.

I was twenty-eight when I made the jump into commercial real estate. Never too young. Never too old. Within ten years, you can accomplish amazing things.

Strategy: Determine where you are, where you want to go, and set a timeline. I don't know about you, but since I love what I do I don't see myself retiring for some time. There is always something new to learn, the thing you wanted to do some day, or a time in your life you want to invest your hard earnings in as a vehicle to *pay it forward* to the next generation.

Myth #14: You must be extremely smart.

Facts: Brain power has nothing to do with it when you believe this fact: A healthy brain can answer any question. The challenge with most people is that they are not quite sure about the questions to ask, which is why we have advisors. Do you know that you get paid directly proportional to the questions you ask and the problems you solve? This is a fact. Your quality of life is also directly proportional to the questions you ask. There are numerous resources for almost anything you need to find out, and it's your resourcefulness that's in question and what makes the difference.

I'm going to sound dumb, but here's the truth . . . I took algebra for over two years in high school, pre-engineering for three years, had a six-year plan for a four-year degree, and failed the PE test four times. Should I go on? I wasn't that smart. I just worked long hours and stood up every time I was knocked down, which was almost every day.

You must act toward getting what you want in your life. You simply need to believe, focus, and work smart.

Strategy: Everything you need is within you NOW. Live in a world of performance. TAKE MASSIVE ACTION, and you will achieve the dream of your life!!

Myth #15: You must have an office and a large staff.

Facts: You don't need an office or a large staff; however, to be effective, you do need a large team (not on the payroll that is) and great office equipment.

You can have several team players to help spread wings on business development and finding deals. For example, tap into brokers, agents, lawyers, architects, and contractors that are on the front line of transactions. You want to keep in mind, as we all know, the cliché "out of sight, out of mind." Tell them what you are looking for, keep their radar in tune, and have them as boots on the ground for you.

Every dime invested in top quality office equipment will pay for itself several times over.

With your team in place, office all set up, and plan ready for execution, you can accelerate progress with use of the Modern Wealth Building Formula. It can either be a hobby or something you get serious about.

Strategy: Buy two sturdy tables or a used desk. Get creative with an L-shape setup or set tables parallel so you can have one behind you to lay out workflow. Connect your laptop wirelessly to the Internet. Set up a dual monitor, printer, and you are good to go.

For what it's worth, if you can overcome these myth beliefs, it's half the battle as these myths all fall under the category of MINDSET—shifting your beliefs, or as the old phrase that many hate hearing goes, *shifting your paradigm.* Once you do that, it's the top-down thinking that will keep you at the top.

Like any sport, be aware that commercial real estate is a highly competitive and adversarial business, and therefore you don't want any myths in your way. While negotiations need not be combative or confrontational, the process nevertheless pits parties with opposing interests against each other and the cream will always rise to the top, especially if you are aware of and focus on those landmines that present themselves along the way. In outlining these myths and strategies to mitigate them, you are better equipped to remove the obstacles and challenges that often plague so many real estate investors.

Luckily for you, I have screwed it up every which way, to the point where I wasn't sure I would fully recover from my mistakes and the endless learning curve. But in writing this chapter, I hope that my setbacks become your opportunities. If you can avoid even a few of these myths and paradigms, you will find yourself starting the race far ahead of the competition. If one man's trash is another man's treasure, then you should cherish this chapter. You can make all your dreams come true, one opportunity at a time.

Imagine yourself at the top of the world, entering an elevator cab with only one button that says, "PH." You push that button and ascend fifty-eight floors where the door opens to the living room in a luxury penthouse looking over Manhattan. It's breathtaking, and your first response is, "Yes, now that's what I'm talking about—*an elevator to the penthouse.*" That is the focus of the final chapter of this book.

The question isn't who is going to let me; it's who is going to stop me.

Ayn Rand, *writer and philosopher*

CHAPTER 11

ELEVATOR TO THE PENTHOUSE:
How to Get There and Stay There

C lose your eyes for a moment.
Do you see it? Feel it?

You are on the elevator, butterflies in your stomach and lightheaded because of the fast-moving velocity of the metal vessel accelerating like a bullet through a gun.

Isn't it great? There you are, headed to the top of the house, the highest and most expensive condo in the entire structure. As the elevator dings and the door opens, you exit directly into your 5,000-square-foot masterpiece. Living in the lap of luxury is the only way to live. After taking a few steps onto the heated marble floor, you throw yourself down on your oversized couch. You then stretch out your back and look out of the floor-to-ceiling windows for a vision of the rest of the world.

You have views of the Empire State Building, Statue of Liberty, and Central Park. As you approach the window and watch the passersby hustling through the Manhattan streets, you can only think of how fortunate and grateful you are to enjoy the relaxed state of your dwelling. It took years to get here, but you have officially arrived.

While this might sound like a dream to many of you, the lessons within this book are the true path to get to the penthouse and stay in the penthouse.

I'm excited as I raise the bulkheads, expand the floor plan horizontally, and combine two converted penthouse rental units into a 10,000-square-foot penthouse extravaganza overlooking Central Park with two private elevators. It's the very top floor with interior living space exceeding 5,000 square feet with a wraparound terrace and terrarium in the living room that encloses a stairway to heaven. It leads to a landscaped paradise with full automation and lighted trellis that covers private dining, kitchen, firepits, recreation areas, and a luxury saltwater spa.

So, while this project will take me eighteen months to complete, I'm writing this final chapter while sitting on a cushioned chair at my partner's penthouse in Myrtle Beach after a round of golf. I can hear the ocean waves crash against the shore with a mild breeze and splash of saltwater energy flowing onto my face. It's at this moment that I reflect on my journey and accomplishment of reaching the final chapter of this book, such that I can leave you with the discovery of the buried treasure as I see it.

There isn't anyone in the world that I'm aware of that has shared the intricacies of success at the highest level of real estate investing: skyscraper development. And I'm happy that I've reached a point in life where I've taken this opportunity to gather my big ideas, my journey, and my lessons to share with you as a road map for your real estate investing journey.

Can you imagine living in one of the highest places in the world? Not only in terms of your living quarters, but being at the top of the world in every area of your life? Living in the penthouse would be just one of the luxuries. The true fulfillment would be your journey from your mastery in life and business as you envisioned it. You would achieve an internal peace and happiness in your relationships. Your priorities would be health, fitness, and spirituality, with a goal to find freedom and learn, all while paying it forward. This would be the culmination of being whole and complete with all matters in life, something that money can't buy.

In other words, you would have accomplished your goals, obtained the toys and material things that your ego may still need, and finally awakened to the fact that it was not about the destination, it was truly about the journey and the lives you changed in paying it forward. This would be the fulfillment of the long-term vision that no one could see when you tried to explain it, or the times you were laughed at for going to those seminar things and the many sleepless nights wondering if you could actually make it . . . and then discovering that you were good enough and could reach any goal you project to the world.

You've heard this a hundred times before and wonder if you believe it could happen where one day you could do what you want, when you want, and how you want in style. This is the ultimate service to your life's purpose with family, friends, and strangers with the realization that you have a gift and can give value to anyone. This is where you can keep it simple and make a choice.

You might choose to wake up each day and throw on a pair of shorts and your favorite T-shirt that says, "Life is good." You might decide to volunteer at a homeless shelter for the day, or spend time giving back at church or building an empire. Whatever it is, my point in sharing all of this with you is that you have arrived. Taking the lessons in this book and implementing them into your savings, your future, and your monthly income can offer you the amazing occasion to live your best life.

The Elevator to the Penthouse

You are on your way to the top. With each passing floor, you near the magnificent penthouse resting at the top of the skyscraper in the middle of your respective city. With each floor passing, you have learned a lesson that has propelled you forward, helping you make it to the top. No one lesson, tip, decision, or investment will get you to the top. Rather, it is the culmination of all the hard work, smart decisions, and strategic investments you've made along the way.

Each of the chapters in this book should assist you in your journey, helping you to reframe your outlook in real estate, investing, and in building a portfolio of opportunities to inject financial resources into your life. I wrote this book after looking back at the years of very late nights rethinking the old traditional approaches to investing. In doing so, I learned that there was one common thread in my derivation of the formula: The stock market has significant ups, downs, and unpredictability. Even in a great market, your gains will often pale in comparison to that of the opportunity we find in a strong real estate market. As economic and investment tides change throughout our generation, real estate remains a viable and constant resource for reliable long-term investments.

If you've been to the beach and swum in the ocean, then you too are familiar with low and high tides. You might have even seen the lifeguards alert swimmers to be aware of the undertow flow. You might have felt the flow of the ocean in an undertow. You can actually feel the water pulling your feet out from under you, the feeling of drifting out to sea as the ocean pulls you away. In the case of undertow, going with the flow could lead to catastrophic consequences. The same can be true in managing or choosing your investment strategies.

Therefore, the perspective I want you to take away is a new outlook on investing—a way to modernize the traditional approach. Combining these elements of traditional investing, we have created the Modern Wealth Building Formula for real estate that is a viable option to secure financial freedom. As the tides rapidly turn, we need to reevaluate our investment system to better understand why people retire broke, even when they are doing all the right things leading up to their later years. This modernized traditional approach can lead you to a successful portfolio, with more time, freedom, and the ability to reap rewards into retirement.

Consider and evaluate your stock investments to determine if your money is invested for maximum profit; and/or if you want to enter an industry with the lowest cost of entry to start a business that can reap unlimited reward, in other words, real estate. The key to this new outlook is your paradigm shift (your way of thinking) so that you can better understand and feel comfortable with the notion that sometimes you might drown if you just go with the flow.

In this book, I have put forth my best effort to help you along the way. After introducing the key themes and concepts in the first chapter, we then discussed the Modern Matrix, a customized real estate approach and strategy for you to either get started or to take your portfolio to the next level. We focused on the Modern Matrix examples of the different types of investors, how it applies to anyone (regardless of their favorite investment strategy), and then worked to understand how the matrix can save time, money, and leave you with a strategy to devour real estate investing.

Remember, the Modern Matrix is not an array of numbers, symbols, or expressions arranged in *rows* and *columns*. Rather, it's an array of the types of real estate investing you have available to you, as well as the levels in which you might want to participate in them. The Modern Matrix applies for any level of an investor, regardless of his or her experience, preferred level of participation, and/or target market sectors. Therefore, regardless of where you are in the process of real estate investing, this matrix is a ready-aim-fire approach with a very specific target in your real estate investing venture.

In Chapter 3, "The Modern Wealth Building Formula," I derived the formula from my life in real estate and found a direct application to business professionals that trade time for money and want their hard-earned dollars working better for them. The formula is for the professional practitioners that include dentists, doctors, lawyers, engineers, and architects, just to name a few. It also applies to employees who want to break free from the constraints of simply cashing a paycheck. Since I didn't want to be one of those unfortunate investors or retirees, I created a formula that shifts your mindset and then sets you up to implement a powerful system to **S**ave **Y**our **S**elf **T**ime, **E**nergy, and **M**oney so that you can create passive income for retirement, security, and peace of mind.

There are two primary components of the Modern Wealth Building Formula:

1. Shifting your paradigm related to investing

2. Implementing a critical three-step process, mentioned next.

In this chapter, we unpacked each of these at greater length, outlining why they are essential for the FIND, FUND, and FACILITATE process to work most effectively.

In Chapter 4, "Commercial versus Residential Real Estate," we focused on the main differences between commercial and residential real estate: the use, management style, and cost. Commercial properties are primarily used for a large range of business types. These investment properties can vary in use, such as medical facilities, office buildings, strip malls, shopping centers, and/or storefronts, just to name a few. Typical commercial property owners invest their money with the expectation to secure a certain return on their investment.

On the other hand, residential properties are typically used to house occupants for a personal residence or property where people pay rent to the owner. Similar to owners of commercial properties, residential owners buy homes to secure a return or live on the property with the hope that the property increases in value. In most cases, these types of investors eventually see the value of their home increase over time. They then figure, "Why not buy another one for financial gain?" And that's typically how it begins. One becomes two, and so on and so forth.

Both commercial and residential real estate can be a valuable part of your portfolio. Choosing the right one should often be based on your lifestyle, financial situation, and retirement goals. Many people have a second home, a two- or four-family dwelling that brings extra income into the primary residence. Either way, there is great opportunity in these investments.

In Chapter 5, "Evaluating the Market," we looked at the market analysis of commercial real estate investments since most comparable market analyses for residential properties are done by real estate agents for free.

Investing in real estate requires certain knowledge of your chosen local markets. Just like coaching a football team, property sellers, property buyers, and landlords all must look at the game as offense, defense, and special teams. The coach can't just focus on offense to be a winner. In real estate, you can't just sit and wait until you are on the field. Always pay attention to the investment properties you are targeting. Take it from my experience, it can be very helpful, and it makes sense if you are establishing your territory. It will provide you with realistic data from hands-on experience about what to expect when you're renting, making an offer on, or listing a property in that market.

In Chapter 6, "Money, Money, Money," we focused on how investors can acquire unlimited funding. In general, there are three simple tips that will unlock the door to it:

Tip #1: Buy Below Market Value. Know the market by following my recommendations on market analysis and find out the median price of your chosen market type for properties in your targeted areas. A realtor or quick Google search can tell you this.

Tip #2: Do Your Homework. Don't expect anyone to take you seriously if you don't do your homework. Like anything, you become an expert after putting in the time and money to understand the market, the investment, and craft a strong strategy.

Tip #3: Negotiate Your Ass Off. Getting the best price means making a smaller deposit and recognizing a greater rate of return. Investors will be attracted to you when they recognize your negotiating skill set. So don't take this lightly.

In Chapter 7, "Ready, Set, Build," rubber met the road. There, we discussed how you can begin to put the wheels in motion to invest in and/or build your own real estate empire. Start small and scale accordingly. Remember that it can take time to build something that lasts, and it is important to be creative. Consider your risk tolerance, and secure the capital that will keep you going.

Are you ready to quit your day job? If so then Chapter 8, "Quit! Your Day Job" is for you. There we discussed how you can turn real estate investing into a full-time business. We discussed the highs and the lows of building your own business, but in the end if you put in the time and effort you will almost certainly build something that truly lasts.

In Chapter 9, "Fee Gold," the challenge that came to mind was how I could generate fee gold at the beginning of the rainbow to enable us to run the business. I structured the deal where we could contract with ourselves to be the developer, which I was not sure how to do at first. So off to my advisors I went. This chapter will help you build a winning team and develop into the king of the hill.

In Chapter 10, "Don't Step in It!" I unmasked the Fifteen Unmistakable Myths of Commercial Real Estate. It doesn't matter what industry or profession you're in—myths happen. I've come to learn there are many misconceptions about real estate in general. Many of these investing myths are simply not true.

This journey has been a labor of love, and in many ways my life's work. To that point, I would go as far as to say that I love real estate more than just about anything in this world other than my family—the ups, the downs, the amazing opportunities. The most important thing for you, the reader, is to make the right choice for you. Whether you are using this book to begin dabbling in the real estate market or as a reference manual or road map to build a real estate empire, your ticket to the top of the penthouse is ultimately a unique and special adventure that is all your own.

I want you to make the right choice today about real estate investing. And that is different for every single person out there. No matter what your needs may be, we have the support team in place to help you execute the Modern Wealth Building Formula curriculum.

For those of you who are indecisive, choose and inquire further about the distinction between a decision and a choice. In short, I'll leave you with a simple explanation where decision is based on reasoning and a choice is what you choose because you choose without reason. You choose real estate because you choose real estate. In our Modern Wealth Building Formula curriculum, we have training available for you to learn exactly how to identify profitable real estate investments, and we consult you through closing deals.

In fourteen weeks or less, we can work together to create a clear investment strategy that matches your financial goals and ideal lifestyle, begin identifying deals to invest in, train you to discover how to use other people's experience and investors' money to execute deals, give you the confidence to manage the whole investment process with minimal risk, and earn additional passive income.

Firsthand, we know this process can be overwhelming for people, even those with a lot of traditional real estate experience. So we provide our clients with system step-by-step training, processes, checklists, and templates to simplify and accelerate the process of building their real estate business.

One of the key things that separates my Modern Wealth Building Formula from other programs is that while we do follow proven processes, we don't lock you into a cookie-cutter approach or prescribe the same strategies to every client. We tailor a program that helps you identify what works for YOU specifically and exactly what's needed to hit your goals.

Finally, we know that starting or growing a business can be lonely and stressful at times, so we deliver ongoing consulting services and community resources to help you reach financial freedom, earn passive income, and build wealth faster than you would alone.

Make the choice NOW about your next step! You can find out more at KenVanLiew.com.

It's time to get your show on the road, and no matter your dreams, aspirations, or just someone you want to help in your life, real estate is a golden opportunity to begin a journey to your Elevator to the Penthouse. Please make every day an outstanding and blessed day in your journey to be extraordinary. It's easy to be ordinary, however it's even more fun and fulfilling to be extraordinary. Bring it on today, TAKE THE ACTIONS NOW, and I'll see you at the top!

Until next time, may your higher spirit bless you with freedom, happiness, and peace of mind as life is too short to dwell on decisions. Choose to BE who you want to be, DO what you want to do, and HAVE an extraordinary and fulfilling experience in the penthouse of life.

QUESTIONS:

- Do I need to be a millionaire to invest in Real Estate?
- Can I invest in Real Estate without experience?
- Do you want to know how to get more time?

ANSWERS:

Sign up for a FREE
45 minute strategy call at
www.kenvanliew.com

ABOUT THE AUTHOR

If Ken Van Liew can make it, so can anyone. His story should inspire people to take actions towards having more time and financial freedom, an extraordinary life, and creating wealth and success through real estate and business. Born in New Brunswick, NJ, Ken was raised middle class, graduated high school and applied for financial aid to attend college with a $10 dollar a week stipend to start his college career.

With a narrow understanding of money, a grid iron mentality from his all-state football honors and a dream for financial success, he struggled through learning math and sciences. After leaving his professional football aspirations on the Division 3 football field, he was accepted into an engineering school three and one half years later.

After another three years and transferring majors, Ken received a hard won bachelor's degree in Civil Engineering. He thought things would become a little easier, but little did he know, the bumpy road didn't end with receiving his degree because he could not pass his professional engineering exam. Several years and five attempts later, Ken finally passed that exam which triggered a light bulb moment for him at age 27 to establish a clear vision and path to fulfillment. Upon this enlightenment, he started with a civil design engineering job, twins and a six-figure debt to increase the burning desire to have total fulfillment.

With his dream intact, relentless perseverance and insurmountable vision for an extraordinary life, three years later, he cut the ribbon on the development of a $17M dollar, 72,000 square feet, 113 bed assisted living facility. He parlayed this success into a Staten Island waterfront development, and began a mastery journey with Tony Robbins. While attending a Tony Robbin's Life & Wealth Mastery event on 9-11 in Hawaii, his waterfront development was terminated due to the World Trade Center collapse. Ken also lost one of his best friends and the $500,000 investment.

On the ropes, he managed to rise again with the development of a New Jersey Transit Village, 240 Park Avenue South, an 18-story, 52 luxury condominiums and a residential private investment fund.

Ken then gambled his second success into three New York City high-rise developments with mezzanine loans held by Lehman Brothers. In 2008, their demise left his development group with millions in losses and three projects that vaporized overnight.

It was at this time in his career that Ken's strength, tenacity and determination capitalized and accelerated. He began attempts to buy Stewart's Root Beer for an international beverage play, created the Ultimate Real Estate Development Academy (formally 8-Figure Deals With No Money and built an online business, all while slowly reentering the real estate game. And it was at this time that Ken realized the 108,000 accumulated hours dedicated to engineering, construction, and real estate development created the highest level of mastery that could have a major impact on people's lives worldwide if he shared his hard won experience and knowledge with other people.

After building a few concrete towers and three hundred more residential high-rise units in New York City, the formula begin to crystalize. At that time in his life, Ken began to see it as his duty to share his experience and knowledge with others to help people get from where they were to where they wanted to go in real estate. And he created the *Modern Wealth Building Formula* as the fastest track to building wealth in real estate.

Author, educator, engineer and one of Manhattan's most successful skyscraper experts, Ken Van Liew has garnered international praise for his work in various facets of the building trades. Starting his real estate career more than a quarter century ago, Ken has gone on to oversee the investment, finance and development phases of numerous large-scale projects, and has a proven track record of successfully handling every aspect of numerous residential, commercial and retail projects. Some of his accomplishments include 1,500 luxury high-rise residential units, a three million square feet commercial office and residential quick turn, and a fix and flip system that has completed over 3,000 transactions.

Over the years, Ken has managed the syndication and development of numerous high-profile real estate investments totaling more than $1.3 billion dollars in capital investment. As an author, Ken is sharing his business experience with readers through his *Modern Wealth Building Formula* and has co-authored books, Secrets *How to Create & Master Clients for Life* and *How to Buy Your Dream Home with Little or No Money Down, Even With Imperfect Credit.* As an educator, he has shared his wisdom with clients of his Real Estate Investing and Wealth Builders Mastermind programs.

As a Professional Engineer, Ken holds Master Degrees in Civil Engineering from the New Jersey Institute of Technology and in Real Estate Development from New York University. In addition, he has lectured at the New York University Real Estate Institute and the College of Engineering at Rutgers University.

Ken is a lifelong student of personal development. He is a Senior Leader in the Tony Robbins leadership organization, Robbins Research International and an Introduction Leader in the performance organization Landmark Worldwide. He has dedicated over 14 years to the Boys Scouts of America as an Assistant Scout Master and Eagle Scout advisor, transforming young men into leaders and is the proud Father of an Eagle Scout and US Marine Intelligence Officer.

A man of enormous gratitude, Ken is most grateful for family, faith and relationships. Married for over 30 wonderful years to his lovely wife Terry, they are the proud parents of three talented and successful children – Alyse, Courtney and Michael. Reflecting his belief that "Giving is receiving," Ken invites you to enjoy his website (www.KenVanLiew.com), intended as his way of expressing his thanks to all those who so generously mentored him along the road to success.

As the well-known Buddhist proverb states, "When the student is ready, the teacher will appear." With that in mind, Ken suggests this may be your time – the day to begin learning his *Modern Wealth Building Formula* with cutting edge techniques and strategies for creating wealth through real estate investing.

For more information about the author and the Modern Wealth Building Formula, visit the website at KenVanLiew.com.

CONNECT WITH KEN AT:

https://www.linkedin.com/in/kenvanliew/

https://www.facebook.com/kenvanliew/

https://www.twitter.com/kenvanliew/

https://www.youtube.com/KenVanLiew

Endnotes

1   "A conversation with W. Chan Kim and Renee Mauborgne" (PDF). INSEAD. 2004. Archived from the original (PDF) on 2008-12-03. Retrieved 2008-12-31.

2   Reference Source: http://42floors.com

3   The results of the Deloitte Global study, "Industry 4.0: Global Human Capital Trends 2018"

https://www2.deloitte.com/content/dam/Deloitte/at/Documents/human-capital/at-2018-deloitte-human-capital-trends.pdf

Made in the USA
Middletown, DE
23 December 2019

81857415R00136